# STARRING MOTHERS

# STARRING MOTHERS

### 3 0  P o r t r a i t s

### o f

### A c c o m p l i s h e d

### W o m e n

. . . .

## PHOTOGRAPHS BY BARBRA WALZ
## INTERVIEWS BY JILL BARBER

*A Dolphin Book*
*Doubleday & Company, Inc. Garden City, New York. 1987*

*With love to our mothers,*

*Pauline Turner and Marjorie Barber*

## Design by Kevin Walz

Library of Congress Cataloging in Publication Data:

Walz, Barbra.
Starring mothers.

"A Dolphin book."
1. Mothers—United States—Interviews.
2. Celebrities—United States—Interviews.   I. Barber,
Jill. II. Title.
HQ759.W335   1987      306.8′743′0922      86-29160
ISBN 0-385-23113-5
ISBN 0-385-23118-0 (pbk.)

# Contents

. . . .

# I N T R O D U C T I O N

INTERVIEW AT
JOYCE CHOPRA'S

BARBRA
NURSING ADDIE
AT EIGHT THOUSAND FEE

LEAVING FOR
MARTHA'S VINEYARD

JILL AND
BARBRA AT THE
GOVERNOR'S MANSION

THE NANNIES
AND NEWBORNS
OF NANCY LOPEZ
AND BARBRA WALZ

TINA WEYMOUTH
PHOTO SESSION

LORIN KLARIS,
PHOTO ASSISTANT

*We were introduced to each other at a dinner party—Barbra was the mother of a three-week-old baby and Jill the mother of a one-year-old. We talked about how important it is not to return to work too soon after the birth of a child. The talk drifted from babies back to work and by the end of the evening we had decided to collaborate on a book about motherhood. We would photograph and interview women in the public eye—mothers who had incredible stories to tell about the struggle of having it all and keeping it all together.*

*How difficult it is to give all to your children. Those early days of breast-feeding and working. Barbra's work required traveling and in order to continue breast-feeding her daughter Jersey she traveled to locations with assistants, camera equipment, nanny, and baby. Jersey had logged sixty-five plane flights in her first year of life. Jill started a new business two months before she became pregnant with Rachel. Her memories are about catching a subway every day with three connections, frantic that she would not be home in time to nurse Rachel.*

*In these times when there are more power lunches than afternoon teas we think it is important to bring thirty women together to talk about the joy, the excitement, and the high of having a baby.*

*It was also important to discuss the lows, the fears, and the doubts we all have. The women we have chosen to photograph and interview are all high achievers and apply the same standards to their mothering as they do to their career.*

*At the halfway point of the book, Barbra and her husband Kevin produced their second child, Addie—which is a story unto itself! Addie and her nanny became the new members of our team, traveling with us through the last hectic months of completing the book.*

*Scheduling was a long and arduous process for all concerned. We built up easy relationships during a year or more of telephoning some of our high-powered interviewees. It took a year to schedule our interview with Mayor Dianne Feinstein of San Francisco because of her work calendar; as we sat down to talk it was all so easy to forget the trials we had gone through.*

*Our first out-of-town assignment was a trip to NASA in Houston. The otherworldness of standing in the simulator of the Challenger and imagining being projected into space was mind-boggling. This is Anna Fisher's work and her interview embodies the message of our book—mothers can do everything!*

*We were honored to be guests of the only woman governor in the United States, Martha Layne Collins of Kentucky. She housed us in our own luxurious quarters on the grounds of the mansion. At breakfast the next morning we held our breath as Jersey sat down to a sumptuous breakfast off crystal and Limoges.*

*We spent many hours aloft traveling all over America. Our biggest adventure was flying in Treat Williams's Piper Seneca to see his neighbor Carly Simon on Martha's Vineyard. On our return journey to the Hamptons the plane developed an oil leak and we had to turn around. The*

RACHEL AND JERSEY
IN ATLANTIC CITY

WATCHING
PATTI LABELLE
AT THE TROPICANA

ADDIE'S
FIRST FLIGHT

EVERYONE
INCLUDING BETTY
WENT TO DONNA KARAN'S

THE WALZES

LAST PHOTO
OF THE BOOK:
ADDIE VISITS
WEYMOUTH KIDS

JILL AND BARBRA
WITH METS STAR
RAY KNIGHT

WAKING UP
AT TREAT'S

DONNA KARAN
DOCKS OUR BOAT

HARRY, JILL,
RACHEL, AND JONAH

BARBRA, JILL,
AND ANNA FISHER
ABOARD SIMULATOR

TREAT LETS
JERSEY "PILOT" PLANE

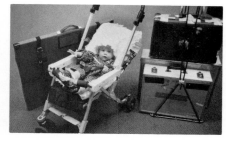

ADDIE AND
EQUIPMENT AT AIRPORT

ADDIE AT BREAKFAST
WITH GOVERNOR COLLINS

party of seven including Barbra's two children became abnormally quiet as we crossed interminable ocean. On landing we had to find a plane to carry us, the baby stroller and three hundred pounds of camera equipment back to East Hampton.

On Labor Day weekend, Jill, Harry, and Rachel walked along the beach from their house on Fire Island to meet Donna Karan and her family in Water Island. Barbra, Kevin, and the girls almost missed their chartered powerboat from Long Island. Longtime friend to both families Ira Sahlman boated us in and out, first by power and then by sail.

After separation from our husbands during too many weekends we decided to make it a family trip to Atlantic City to see Patti LaBelle. Ten of us played on the beach and boardwalk before we met with Patti and her son Zuri. That night the only person who left the casino with any money in his pocket was Jill's husband Harry.

Tina Weymouth worked fast to produce another child while the book was being written. We loved having the excuse to see her again and to introduce baby Egan to baby Addie.

After all the scheduling, traveling, shooting, and interviewing we sifted through some fifteen hundred photographs and nine hundred pages of transcripts to produce this book. It has been an incredible experience delving into the relationship between mother and child, and mother and career. Every interview revealed surprises. We can now share them with you.

Barbra Walz and Jill Barber

# AMY IRVING
. . . .

*Amy Irving was born in Palo Alto, California, to actress Priscilla Pointer and the late Jules Irving, director of the Repertory Theater of Lincoln Center. Her career has moved between the Irvings' tradition of Broadway stage and a West Coast world of Hollywood movies. She made her film debut in Brian de Palma's* Carrie, *and since then she has starred in such movies and TV miniseries as* The Fury, Honeysuckle Rose, The Far Pavilions, *and* Yentl, *for which she received an Academy Award as Best Supporting Actress. On Broadway, her performances in* Heartbreak House *and* Amadeus *received enthusiastic reviews. She married director Steven Spielberg in 1985. They have a son, Max.*

I finally realized what "broody" meant when I played a pregnant woman in the film *Micki and Maude*. A friend told me I wore a determined expression off the set, as if I were going to sit on a nest and defend it against all comers. After each day of shooting, I arrived home with pictures of my swollen belly to show Steven how cute I looked. We wrapped up the film in June; I was pregnant by September. By that time, Steven had the same preoccupied look I did. He wanted someone to share his toys with.

My final weeks of pregnancy coincided with the beginning of shooting for Steven's film *The Color Purple*. On the last day of my pregnancy, I called Steven on the set to let him know I was in labor. He ran to the phone from the middle of filming a dramatic childbirth and I told him—very calmly—"Honey, now come and direct my delivery." He was one of the best Lamaze coaches the method has ever seen.

I had a twenty-three-hour birth. We did it together: myself, Steven, my mother and sister, and Steven's mother. Steven led the pack. He assigned my mother to the back-rubbing tennis ball and his mother to morale raising. The energy in that room was

electric. My mother and sister had their kids by C section, but we were hoping for a natural childbirth here. In the end, the doctors lost the baby's heart rate and they rushed me into another room for a forceps delivery. It was still the best day of my life.

During the hours and hours of minute-and-a-half-long contractions, Steven held my hand, talked me through the contractions, and took me away from the pain. The bond between us felt as important and rich as the childbirth itself. It had the impact of physical force.

Two weeks later, we were on location for *The Color Purple*, and Max was on a diet of mother's milk and bugs. Our priorities had changed: Above all, the family had to stay together. Since then, I've read scripts and asked, "Is this good enough to take me away from my family or to take Max away from Steven?" Steven's decisions have become family-oriented: "What film can we all be together for? What film will I want Max to see?" It's all compromise.

Currently, Steven stays home five days every week and I can't get him back to work. I'm no different. I originally thought I would be like my mother, who had three children and ran back onstage after each one in no time at all. I'd breast-feed for three months and then go to work. But, like Steven, I'm finding the return difficult. I haven't ever felt this fulfilled—and I was extremely content as an actress. I used to be pretty wild, but I haven't had a drink since pregnancy and I'm healthier and happier than ever.

I want another child as soon as possible because we'd like two children close together, and eventually a third, and I know how much work that is going to take. I didn't grow up with a family-oriented lifestyle and now that I'm lady of the house, I have to organize a payroll: a live-in couple, a cook, a mother's helper. We have two houses to look after during the week, and on weekends we hit the beach on Friday nights and come back on Sunday— just the three of us—and I prepare the food and do the dishes.

There is still brooding mixed in with the elation. After three

3
· · · ·

months or so, I began to be a little less enthusiastic about each day. We'd have someone over for dinner and I'd feel insecure about my contribution to the conversation. If they weren't talking about babies, mothers, or schools, I wasn't interested. Instead, I turned blue. It wasn't hormones—I finally realized I'd been breast-feeding Max since birth and I was burned-out.

I do think hormonal changes occur when you give up some of your breast-feeding. After all, your baby is losing his total dependence on you. When Steven gave him that first bottle, I cried, and Steven said, "Oh, great. What are you going to be like on his first day of school?"

I've even had trouble coping with advice. During the last few months of pregnancy, Steven would call me and pass on tidbits: "So-and-so said to sandpaper your nipples to prepare for nursing." Stupid me: I'd diligently scrub with a fine-grade abrasive, wincing and wondering how I was ever going to be able to breast-feed. Shortly afterwards our Lamaze tutor told me to put lanolin on my nipples. I couldn't listen to all of those people.

Steven and I did pay attention to everything Dustin Hoffman had to say because he has had so many kids. I figured I would get a nurse to take care of Steven, and I would take care of the baby, but Dustin said, "You know what's nice? A night nurse who will bring you the baby when it wakes up for a feeding in bed."

I am finally reading scripts again. I would love to go back to New York and perform in a limited-run play because I prefer the theater. The theater schedule is more of a strain, but after rehearsals, you perform at night while the baby's asleep. But if Max is in school, I'll be inflexible. I'm not going to yank him out of the classroom for a plane bound for New York.

I just finished *Rumpelstiltskin,* a fairy-tale musical for Cannon Films. My brother directed, I played the Miller's Daughter, and Max became the First-Born Son. He had the same role I played when my mother was the Miller's Daughter and my father Rumpelstiltskin.

*Dianne Feinstein became the mayor of San Francisco on November 27, 1978, after Mayor George Moscone was shot and killed. She has since won elections in 1979 and 1984, and turned the city's $127 million deficit into a $152 million surplus. She successfully lobbied the federal government for $46 million to rehabilitate the cable car system, and crime and unemployment have declined. Her firm leadership is well known. Her daughter Catherine is a deputy district attorney in San Francisco.*

Americans like to believe that combining motherhood and career is guaranteed success under the American Dream—work hard enough and you can do anything. That is not realistic! I've worked through the worst of circumstances—alone with a small child and no help, and later, after the death of my second husband, I kept on working, alone again. I worried about money and economic security, and I've learned that the problems won't end when you're financially secure. Whether you work to survive or work for yourself, your children still have needs.

Most of today's professionally oriented women will begin to want a family, and having decided that, they'll grapple with this issue. When a child is young, you pull yourself from the workplace to the home. A home is birthday parties, Christmas dinner, and Halloween. It's three of your child's friends spending the night over, and it's sickness, staying up all night to nurse her through. You have to make yourself available for the school party or the PTA.

My daughter is a deputy district attorney. Can she have three children and continue to work when she has hundreds of active cases, leaves the house at 7 A.M., and doesn't return home until seven at night? I've tried to help by telling her I'll be there as a grandmother, pitching in, but she has to work it out herself. She'll have to be willing to set aside most things in her life beside her work and her husband to be able to come home and be with her child. We'd like to place that responsibility on a housekeeper, baby-sitter, counselor, or child-care center. We can't. We must provide the intensive attention children need. They need to have a sense of authority and discipline. They need to be taught how to give and receive love. I have no doubt that if Catherine were small, I couldn't be the mayor of a big city and still carry out the obligations—and enjoy the pleasures—of motherhood.

When I had Catherine in the 1950s, there was no such thing as a maternity leave. I lost my job. Every night at seven, I put Cathy to sleep and then the walls closed in around me. When I did find a job, I served on the California Women's Board of Terms and Parole for ten days out of thirty and the rest of the month I was free for Cathy. Still, it wasn't easy. When a child says "Mama," it doesn't want Mama three days from then.

I put many career moves on hold. For example, from the time I was sixteen, I knew I wanted to run for the Board of Supervisors. I had an uncle who'd take me down to what he called "The Board of Stupidvisors" and he'd say, "You go out, get an education, come back and do this job." I knew that was what I wanted to do. But it was never economically feasible. Nor could I reconcile it with being a parent, until I met my second husband, Bert Feinstein. He enabled me to work by helping with Cathy and staying at home while I was away, and he loved doing it.

I can't stress how important the right man, the right husband, is when you're working. It helps if he isn't in a comparable job because he needs to be secure in whatever he does; the woman can't be a threat. You, of course, have to be flexible in return.

I don't have easy answers for my daughter and all the others contemplating a family. Keep control of your professional life. If you determine your own schedule, life will be much easier. Be patient with your career and know the special, devoted attention a young child demands will eventually pay off.

Good day care helps. I was part of a cooperative nursery school and, in those days, the mother contributed one morning a week to the program. I helped in the center; I even cleaned johns. Nursery school was a positive experience for both of us. Still, you'll want to be there to hold a crying child for as long as it takes despite the best day care in the world.

Emphasize the hours when you're not exhausted, the moments you can give completely to your children and their pursuits. If children sense that undivided attention, those special hours, they will be willing to turn around and be interested in your life and all the pressures you face. Keep your children on your side.

I've tried very hard to reach that understanding with Catherine. There's never been a question in her mind that I care very much about how she is and the help she needs—despite all the bad times. We had a bomb at the house and a shot through the window and Catherine has wanted to reject any connection I've had with the public arena. Despite it all, we reached the moment when she said to me, "I want to thank you for all those nights you stood at the head of the stairs in your flannel nightgown with your arms folded, waiting for me to come home."

I worry that women with a career will forget how important family life is. You reach a point in your life when family has died, few are left, and then you really begin to treasure the memories you've stored through the years, the time you had while they were here.

Finally, simply, if I hadn't had a child, I'd never have known that most elemental, direct, true relationship. I don't know if I'd fully understand the values of society that I prize. I would have missed some of the mystery of life and death. Not to know how a child grows, the wonder of a newborn's hand . . . I have been fortunate.

9

*Donna Karan enrolled in Parsons School of Design and in her second year found a summer job with Anne Klein, the legendary fashion designer. She remained with Anne Klein as her right-hand assistant and, after Anne's death in 1974, took over as principal designer for the line. Donna formed her own company, Donna Karan New York, in 1984 and immediately became New York's newest fashion superstar. She is married to Stephan Weiss, a sculptor, and has a daughter, Gabrielle.*

I was always working. At six o'clock in the morning of Gabrielle's birth, I was told, "You better come over here and get your designs into work." At that moment, I was filling out paperwork for the production of some of my clothes. I replied, "Excuse me, but I'm going into contractions." Later that day, I began hard labor and I went to the hospital. I delivered in the morning, and my boss called in the afternoon to ask, "When are you coming back to work?" I said, "What? Don't you want to know if I had a girl or a boy? Doesn't anyone care about my baby?"

In the hospital, I sat in a yoga position with a small tape recorder that played "The First Time Ever I Saw Your Face." Every mother has a song with her child, something that's played during that magical time in the hospital. The phone rang. "You've got to come to work!" my boss said. I replied, "There is no conceivable way I'm coming in. My doctor won't let me out." It was the beginning of March, a cold and stormy day, and my doctor was afraid of the germs I'd bring back with me. My boss called back and said, "Well, if you're not coming back to work, we're coming to you."

Our house was new, empty, and deserted. I moved in with Gabrielle. A truck arrived from New York with racks and racks of the new collection followed by most of the people in the organization. I thought it was going to be a party until I received one more call. Anne Klein had died that morning. A birth and a

death within the same week. I attended her funeral and then I began to assemble the fall collection. I felt terrible, having a child, and working long hours to essentially start a business from scratch.

I now need the counterbalance of a child. This is not a glamorous profession at all. It's hard work, dedication, tremendous headaches, and you're only as good as your last collection. My family fulfills other facets of my personality. I have a strong maternal instinct. I treat my business as if I were its mother. I treat the people I work with as a mother would.

Guilt is an emotion that runs far beyond the ramifications of not having enough money for your child. I recently said that I would probably be a guilty mother until the day I die. It's not necessarily healthy for Gaby to know I'm vulnerable. She plays it to the hilt. We were in school together and she said, "My mommy is always working. My mommy is always traveling. Oh, Mommy, are you going to be here for all the events?"

I find it difficult to balance the private moments—the talks together in her room, the weekends and the nights—with my work. It's not easy to be as large a part of your daughter's childhood as you'd want if you're career-oriented. I almost feel as if my dedication was forced on me as opposed to a free choice.

Currently, the work day is endless. I work fourteen hours, most of them spent in meetings where we determine our designs. Fortunately, the phone stops after hours. The staff packs up. Gaby calls to tell me I'm wanted for dinner.

I resented my mother for working. I wanted her there when she wasn't. I did like growing up independent, but I longed for her

presence. Gaby has similar feelings. I said to her once, "You wanted me to be home and now you want to go out. What am I supposed to do, go and wash the laundry?" "I just want to know you're here," she said.

I bring to my daughter love and warmth. Generosity. She enjoys the stimulation I receive from my work. I'm alive, I'm never boring. I'm not jaded or pretentious. I am bothered by the dollar-and-cents value the world puts on celebrity. Gaby has learned a certain amount of materialism from other people telling her that her mother is rich and famous. I hope it's just a stage she's going through.

I'm divorced and remarried, and Gaby adores my husband, Stephan Weiss, whom I've been with now for many years. I originally married my best friend; after the divorce, I went back to my first love. He has two children by a previous marriage, and at first my relationship with Cory and Lisa was very strained. Nothing I did was right, absolutely nothing. I finally broke through when they saw how happy their father was. They began to realize I'd be there for them. I saw them through the difficult time, the teenage years when I thought the house would topple. One day, Cory would move in, and the next, Lisa would move out. They shifted constantly, and Gaby was the sole stable element in the house. The interactions, though, were actually good for Gaby. She adores Lisa. She looks like Lisa. She talks like Lisa. She secretly thinks deep down in her heart that Cory is wonderful too, but, of course, he's a boy.

Every woman should have a child. The sense of loss must be painful for those without a maternal relationship. There's nothing more warm and sensitive than a child. You complete the full range of emotions. For me, that's what living is all about.

15
. . .

# DR. ANNA FISHER

*Dr. Anna Fisher was selected by NASA for astronaut training in 1978. As a member of the shuttle mission that in 1984 retrieved two satellites in a "space salvage" mission, she logged 192 hours in 127 orbits around the earth. Her husband, Dr. William F. Fisher, is also an astronaut. They live in Houston, Texas, with their daughter, Kristen. Dr. Fisher graduated from UCLA cum laude with honors in chemistry. She specializes in emergency medicine.*

I certainly thought about my daughter the night before my launch but I actually worried more six months before the mission than I did during the final weeks. I concentrated on my work. The other crew members depended on my performance. I had to focus on the task at hand. The hardest time for Kristen was my first flight on a T-38 jet trainer. It wasn't easy for her to see me go up in the air alone.

Prior to the Challenger explosion, Kristen took launches very much for granted because her friends' parents are also astronauts. My husband and I have always accepted the risk these flights have. It's what we're here for. The accident has alerted NASA to problems in the hardware and we're working hard to see it doesn't happen again. The worst part of the aftermath has been what's happening to NASA. You know the old saying; kick a dog when it's down.

I had to explain to Kristen that the shuttle had blown up and the people on board wouldn't be coming back. She knew the daughter of Mike Smith, the Challenger's commander, very well. Kristen was in school during the explosion; but of course she saw it many times on television.

Luckily, I don't suddenly switch from being a mother to becoming an astronaut. Before my mission, activity only gradually built up. Toward the end, she became very used to my leaving early in the morning and not getting home until late at night. I went into

*18*

quarantine a week before, and the mission lasted a week, and so I was gone only two weeks. She has a wonderful relationship with my mother and her grandparents, and we had a strong family-support structure there to watch over her. She also loves what her mother and father are doing. Her first words were ''Mummy'' and ''Daddy'' and her next word was ''jet.'' I've tried to watch every landing with her, and she has books on the space program.

The decision to have Kristen wasn't easy. I didn't tell NASA I was pregnant for a long time. I thought it might cost me the flight I wanted, but it turned out not to matter. If I'd waited until after my flight, I would have been thirty-six. I didn't have the time to wait. My ground assignment at the time involved constant travel between Houston and the Cape in a jet trainer. NASA would never knowingly let a pregnant woman fly a jet. They'd have been held responsible if we had been hurt in an ejection or accident. I was four and a half months pregnant before I told them. They decided to let me continue since at the time I was the astronaut

in charge of that particular program. I took commercial flights
and I worked until I went into labor.

I don't feel a conflict between my work and my family. If
anything, it's a nice blend. I remember having a lot of fun in the
simulator trying to handle all the emergencies they were giving us
and thinking that in a half hour I'd go home and see Kristen. It's
a stimulating change of pace to share two ways of life, the
technological and the nurturing. I stay busy; there's no time to sit
around and worry about myself.

Having Kristen helps with the shock I feel over Challenger. We
were out driving one day and Kristen noticed a billowing, white
cloud that looked like the explosion. She pointed it out to me and
we talked about what the loss of the Challenger's crew meant. I
find myself these days with more time for her. There's no place
in the world I would rather be than home with Kristen.

# BEVERLY JOHNSON

· · · ·

*Beverly Johnson is one of the world's foremost fashion models. Her career caught fire after she became* Vogue's *first black cover model in 1974. Since then she has appeared on countless magazine covers and in many television commercials. In her film debut she costarred in the movie* Ashanti *with Michael Caine. She has recorded an album,* Don't Lose the Feeling, *and written a book,* Beverly Johnson's Guide to a Life of Health and Beauty. *She has a daughter, Anansa.*

I named my daughter Anansa after the princess I played in my first movie, *Ashanti.* The film was shot in East Africa and I had no idea I was pregnant when I flew to Africa to begin work. I kept my pregnancy a secret during almost the entire production. Wardrobe wondered why they had to keep letting my dress out.

A bad-tempered camel finally revealed my secret. We were in the middle of the Sinai Desert. I had to do a mourning scene, weeping while sitting on a camel in the middle of a caravan. I refused to get up on the animal and the director finally said, "Look, you won't have to move with the camera. Just sit there." The first camel in the caravan stood up, my camel rose, but the one behind us didn't, pulling my saddle off and throwing me into a high rocky gully. It was like falling out of a two-story building. I tried not to land on my head and I went down sitting. The water broke when I hit the ground. I thought I had lost my child. I began to scream. The crew screamed back, "What baby? Oh God, she's pregnant!" Fortunately, the baby was fine, but I was too bruised to even walk.

Anansa was born one month before a twenty-one-country promotional tour for the movie and it devastated me to leave her behind. I wanted to cancel the tour, but my husband wouldn't let me; I was in a Svengali relationship. I was in my twenties, he was in his fifties, and he thought he knew better. When I came back, Anansa was so much bigger. My grandmother, who was taking care of her, said, "She's done this, she's done that." I felt she wasn't even the same baby.

A child had brought responsibility and focus into my life and I saw much more clearly. My husband and I began proceedings and the next two years were the darkest period of my life. Anansa was two years old. We lived in hotels, like vagabonds. My peak modeling years were underway and I had to work. I left Anansa in Buffalo with my mother while I struggled to put my life together. I told myself I had to be Job, I had to be patient, but at the same time I was in court with the worst kind of mudslinging divorce. I read the Bible, passages and proverbs. I wrote songs. I wanted a moment of stillness, of peace. I surrounded myself with family and friends, trying to wrap myself in their love. I couldn't work. The pretty pictures meant nothing to me. I couldn't smile.

Most models would never have a child during their peak years. It's not easy recovering. Thinness is a model's bread and butter. My doctor told me I wouldn't lose any weight until my organs shrank and moved into normal position. Nine months after

pregnancy, I began to diet. I followed my mother's old remedies. I began to wear a girdle. I slept belly down to flatten my stomach. My exercise routine came from my book. It all helped.

Anansa has her own celebrity stature because of interviews I've done, the covers for *Parents' Magazine,* and my exercise book. We've never cultivated it because she isn't patient enough for modeling. Anansa loves to swim and she has been swimming competitively since she was four. She practices every day for an hour and it takes her away from the "Oh, you're pretty" syndrome.

I was worried my ex-husband wouldn't be a parent, and I tried to enforce his presence by the courts. That proved to be a mistake, and I've been in the courts since then, trying to modify our joint custody. Anansa has dealt with the divorce very well. She loves both of us. My lawyer says she's never had a case in which the children didn't say they wanted to live with both parents. Anansa relishes having two homes, two bicycles, two vacations. Who can blame her?

# T I N A  W E Y M O U T H

*Tina Weymouth and her husband Chris Frantz met at the Rhode Island School of Design. With David Byrne, a fellow student, they formed the rock group Talking Heads. In 1976, Talking Heads signed with Sire Records and since then they have recorded six albums of some of the most imaginative popular music in America. Their last two albums have gone platinum and in 1985 they released a concert film,* Stop Making Sense. *Tina and Chris have formed a companion band, Tom Tom Club, which has had two very successful albums. They have two children—Robin and Marshall Egan.*

I never worried about touring while I carried Robin. After all, Nina Hagen had toured through her fifth month and Grace Jones had toured through her sixth. I went on the road avoiding bad vibes just like I'd avoid a cold. I quit smoking and staying up late. I wore a special girdle with lacing in the center. It held the stomach and supported my back. My only problem was vanity; I didn't want to look all blimped out on stage.

I was really going around the world with two children. In 1981, Chris and I started the Tom Tom Club as a counterpoint to the Talking Heads. If Talking Heads was the neurotic first child that you have to deal with, Tom Tom Club was the easygoing, happy-dispositioned baby who never presented a problem. It was a wonderful tour, and in Japan, four months into my pregnancy, Tom Tom Club was actually overshadowing Talking Heads. I had no trouble performing even though David wanted a stand-by bass player in the wings and Jerry wanted me to go on sabbatical altogether. We would run on stage at exactly eight o'clock and the baby would kick during the first three songs before falling asleep.

I performed through the seventh month and intended to have the last two months as quiet time, but somehow I ended up spending the last few days before his birth recording the bass on the LP

*Speaking in Tongues.* Bahamian babies usually pop out just after the water breaks, so they were very surprised when I started contractions at midnight and still had not delivered my baby by 5:30 A.M. The doctor was so shocked he broke my water. I wanted to be in a crouched position and the night nurse wouldn't let me sit up. I finally screamed, "Crank the bed up! Am I supposed to push lying flat on my back? Haven't you heard of gravity?" Now I was allowed to push and I was exhausted.

Well thank god the daytime midwife nurse hoisted the bed, gave me little handles to grip, and bang bang bang, I had the baby.

I thought I would be a terrible mother. I sowed my wild oats for a considerable length of time and knocked myself up the first time I ever made love. I was seventeen, Catholic, a student at Barnard in New York City, and the boy was a university student. I had to decide whether to kill myself or terminate the pregnancy. I later found out that pregnancy is behind over half the female teenage suicides in this country. My mother had told me, "If you get pregnant, I'll raise the child as my own." In retrospect, I wonder why I didn't do that, but at the time, all I could think was, "I want this boy out of my life. I don't want him coming for his child after we raised it." Obviously, I didn't have the maternal instinct.

I decided I was doomed to be bad and so I became an artist. Independence was important. I swore I'd never rely on a man for anything other than romance.

But years later, I knew by the age of thirty I'd have a baby. I wasn't far off the mark. It took Chris a long while to come around to the idea; he kept saying, "I'll be a terrible father," but he stood with me in that Bahamian hospital during the birth and I was glad.

I kept Robin by me in the hospital so he never fell into the habit of crying and it wasn't until he was about a year old that he saw other children cry and began to imitate them. Before this, he only cried when he was hungry or in pain. I wanted to raise him

27

. . . .

Oriental fashion. The Chinese will never allow children to cry; they always pick them up.

The first year of his life I hardly slept because I stayed up with him at night, following this no-crying philosophy. He was convinced he needed his mother's breast to go to bed and if he woke up at three in the morning, he'd think, "Where's Mother? I've got to get back to sleep." I had to harden myself. We were on tour and I was exhausted. I'd thought he'd cry right through the next two weeks, but three minutes of crying would release the tension he was feeling and he'd quickly tire and fall asleep.

We bought this house for Robin. If it weren't for Robin, we would never have moved out of New York; not because we love the city, but because we love the intensity. I grew up in the country and it seems important to me that a child can sit on the ground and play in the dirt. Everything else seems easy because, as my parents say, "He's more adjustable than you are." Robin travels very easily and he loves music.

28

The name of my second boy came to me in a dream. Marshall is a family name and Egan is Celtic. This time around, motherhood is much easier—I go by my instincts. Chris and I are much more relaxed and ready for the responsibility. We feel like a real family.

Luckily, I have a lot of free time and I can be with the children without having to send them off to preschool. Robin is bound for kindergarten next year even though I understand the experts say you should wait until a child's permanent teeth come in because then the child should be old enough to reason logically. Is that how the Age of Reason began?

I talked to Robin once about the time he swam in my tummy. "The walls were red," he said. Now if you are pregnant, the intense light of a Caribbean island will shine through the wall of your stomach. Children remember things from before they are born. I have a friend who said that his mother played the harp when she was pregnant and now whenever he hears the harp, he immediately fills with happiness. I hope Robin feels the same way about the Talking Heads.

# N A N C Y  L O P E Z

*Nancy Lopez was twelve when she won the New Mexico Women's Open. She turned professional after her sophomore year of college and as a twenty-one-year-old rookie in 1979 won nine tournaments, including a record five in a row. After being named both Rookie and Player of the Year, her second season set an LPGA stroke average record until she surpassed it in 1985. She has earned more than $165,000 in each of her seasons since 1978, helping her become the game's youngest millionaire. She married baseball star Ray Knight in 1982. They have two children, Ashley and Erinn.*

Baseball kids have a rough life. When we watch one of Ray's night games, I end up feeding Ashley and Brooks breakfast at noon, just so they know what breakfast is. Sometimes they wake up at one in the afternoon, have breakfast, and then wait for dinner.

Ashley and Erinn travel with me. Golf is a much easier sport on young children. When Ray's team goes on tour, he can't possibly have a child along. I can decide to play a tournament one week and stay home the next. I was the first woman player on the circuit to bring a child along. You need a nanny. Fortunately, I have the financial resources to bring one along.

On the typical tour, I'll put Ashley to sleep at nine and I'll go to bed at ten and get up at eleven. Unfortunately, when I first went on tour with Ashley, she didn't sleep at night. Because of my fears before a tournament I told the nanny that she would have to take the child at night. But when the crying started, it was me who was down the hall to take care of Ashley. I decided to just let her sleep in my room. I normally needed lots of sleep during golf tournaments, but I learned to play through without it.

I'm looking forward to touring with Erinn. She's the exact opposite of Ashley in her sleep patterns. I put her down about ten o'clock and she won't wake up until five-thirty in the

morning. Then I feed her and she sleeps until ten or eleven.

Ashley owns a set of plastic clubs that she can swing around and she has real golf togs. Whenever she's ready, I'll teach her to play. If she likes to play, I'll take her on the course.

Baseball is much harder on the children. Once Ray starts the season, he's in prison. When he has night games he has to sleep the next day, go back to the park, and travel to the next stadium. If the children go to watch a night game, they're out until after midnight. If they don't want to watch the game they can go to the gameroom where the team keeps a baby-sitter.

Even if I can travel with children on the tour, I plan to retire at thirty-four and have a third child. Ashley will be in school then and I don't want to leave here. I really will wait another five years and plan the third child very carefully. Right now, Ashley and Erinn are good ages to be together. To have three and be working and playing the way I am now would be too much. I don't want to put my family aside. God gave me this talent and I can't cheat myself. But I'm going to try for a little boy. Ray says if we don't have a boy we'll keep trying. We're hoping.

It hasn't been easy, having children in the middle of a career. I often feel guilty, but Ray tells me I'm fulfilling needs I have to fulfill. In the beginning of our marriage, I saw how good Ray was with his son Brooks and I wanted to have children. I wanted to share that with him. His divorce put him through so much pain— he missed his son desperately. I had hoped that if we had children it wouldn't be so hard for him to be away from Brooks.

I asked him if he wanted to go back to his first wife because as much as I cared for him, I hated seeing him that miserable. Fortunately, we solved our struggles.

Brooks's mother now has custody of him. Unfortunately, we both travel and the court won't let him be with us. Today, however, Ray has a family to come home to all of the time. He would drop anything for us, just as I would drop my career for my children and husband.

33
. . . .

*Tina Brown, editor-in-chief of* Vanity Fair *magazine, is famous in England as the woman who saved* Tatler, *the world's oldest magazine. As its twenty-five-year-old editor, Tina Brown transformed* Tatler *into a witty chronicler of England's well-to-do and tripled its circulation. Currently, she is performing a similar feat with* Vanity Fair. *Tina Brown has written two books,* Loose Talk *in 1979 and* Life as a Party, *a collection of her profiles for the* Tatler. *She and her husband, Harold Evans, have a son, George Frederick.*

Just before I left England I felt depressed because I didn't feel ready to have a child. All my girlfriends were making me feel part of a terrible soap opera. I was always being talked to, taken to one side at parties and told "surely it is time." I always intended to have a child, but a child was on my long-term agenda. My post-baby depression was all about why didn't I have a baby earlier? Why did I leave it so long? Suddenly it seemed the most important thing in the world that I nearly missed.

Women feel that they have worked very hard for what they have got and they are worried that somehow they will be changed by the hormonal thing of pregnancy. I was afraid I would lose my work drive if I had a baby. I was protecting myself from turning into this great cow, who would lose all ambition and just stay home and cuddle my baby all day long.

We don't know how resourceful we are until we have a child. It is such a basic instinct to accommodate a child into one's life.

America was a revelation. I realized here I could be an executive and still have a child. An English woman's initial flurry of activity subsides when she starts a family. Happily, her American counterpart knows that if you're serious about what you're doing, you'll find a way to continue your career. I'm as driven as I ever was, but now I have something else in my life.

As the months went by, I grew enormously pregnant; I've never seen anyone as vast as myself. I felt wonderful and I continued to work on into the fall. November and December in New York are extremely hectic, and I ran from place to place to keep up with business meetings and lunches. I overworked; I attempted too much. Pregnancy is a very delicate time.

On a Saturday night in January, I began to hemorrhage. My obstetrician told me to have an ambulance take me to Mount Sinai Hospital where he would be waiting. The ambulance crew informed me that Mount Sinai was out of their jurisdiction. I went to New York Hospital where I waited for an hour and a half, not knowing who would deliver my baby. Finally a high-risk obstetrician arrived. I had gone through many expensive obstetricians and for the actual birth I had an unknown doctor. She turned out to be wonderful and performed an instant cesarean. My child promptly went into an incubator for the next month.

36

I felt violated because my child had suddenly been torn from me in the dead of winter instead of being born in April. I was bitter, extremely guilty about overworking, and during my postpartum depression, I mourned the three months at home I thought I was going to have with my child. Instead, I had an unscheduled month's maternity leave with no child to take care of. George spent that time in an incubator with breathing problems. At least, he had been delivered at the proper hospital. New York Hospital is one of the finest preemie centers in the world. I was haunted by what could have happened; my obstetrician seemed to think it was all right to fly to the bitter end. I might have been on the shuttle to Washington.

George couldn't come out of the incubator for feeding. I did express my milk for a month, but I soon dried up. Fortunately, he preferred the bottle. I missed the emotional attachment of feeding. It had always been in my picture of having a child.

George Frederick Evans has a very solid English name because he was born in America. I'd love for him to have an English sort of nursery life, a sweet and unspoiled quality to childhood that is more common over there. At some point, I might look into an English nanny to help create that kind of home environment. I'd like to keep him English, but living in America.

I've realized I'm a workaholic who needs something else in her life. I'd work all the time if I didn't have a child. I used to eat breakfast standing up and spend the evening on telephone call after telephone call until I discovered I had worked for hours. Today, it's a disaster if I can't see George before he goes to bed. I never travel. I hate to go out.

I take care of George myself on weekends and I find work on Monday to be a respite. After a weekend, I'm exhausted and I haven't used my brain the entire weekend except perhaps to snatch a few paragraphs from the Sunday *Times.* Full-time mothering is a tremendously hard job; the heroic women who do it nonstop are to be applauded.

My English friends are staggered that I've gone on working. I think they're a bit disapproving. The English press implies that a working mother can only succeed by neglecting her child, but I'm an extremely doting parent. I'm not there all the time, but I'm all over him when I am. In some ways, an office job means that you can concentrate on your work there and devote yourself totally to your child when you come home.

My managing editor has a new baby. She literally walked two blocks to the Brooklyn Hospital and had a bouncing baby on July 4 with fireworks going off outside. She worked throughout her pregnancy, without any problems. My production editor is pregnant. Both these women are devoted to their jobs. They will become more resourceful about the way they handle their work and I think we have to be a bit tolerant of that. They will find a way to do it and be good mothers. The company we work for is enormously elastic and as long as you get your work done no one is going to ask whether you are there at nine o'clock. As long as the figures are great, then nobody will ask where you are.

I was never someone who leapt out of bed at six-forty, but I'm up and about early in the morning to take care of George and have a few hours with him before I start work. I try to get home by no later than five forty-five in order to have a few more hours with him. My day is now much more calibrated to free that time. I sometimes feel it's too exhaustively measured and organized, but I wouldn't trade for my old life at all. I never bother going to anything between six and eight now, because I must be able to see him before he goes to bed. If there is something I must do at that time I make sure I can get home between three and four somehow. So far I haven't missed anything.

Having a baby is like falling in love again, both with your husband and your child. My husband and I have found the experience extremely romantic. George is a tremendous bond between us. With George, I wait for a smile, feeling like I'm standing by the phone, hoping for a call. I also find that motherhood connects you to other women, creates an instant common interest. I tend to be absorbed in my own obsessions; motherhood breaks me free.

If you're in your mid-thirties and uncertain about a family, have your child. Adjust afterwards. Your baby will make you much more sensitive and open. You won't harden. You'll relearn the world through your child's eyes.

George's great passion is trees. He loves to lie on his back and stare up into the branches. It's wonderful to feel his tremendous excitement about parts of our lives that normally go unnoticed. I now walk about with my eyes open. I'm always looking for a tree for George.

*Lindsay Wagner won an Emmy for her 1975–78 show* The Bionic Woman. *Her television roles include among many others* Scruples, Callie & Son, I Want to Live, *and the ABC series* Jessie. *She also starred in the Oscar-winning film* The Paper Chase. *Off camera, she champions such causes as prevention of child abuse, coping with learning disabilities, and holistic medicine. She and her son Dorian live on the Salmon River near Mount Hood, Oregon.*

Pregnancy meant a choice—I could drop my career and go live in the mountains, or I could work harder than I ever had before to secure my finances. In the next two years, I accomplished more than I ever had in any comparable period of my career and the baby was with me the whole time.

From the day of conception, I felt stronger, as if a declaration had been made. I became much more careful about avoiding negative energy. I read, followed advice, and continually worked on maintaining a healthy, positive attitude.

Guidance came from the American Holistic Medical Association for whom I've done a lot of publicity over the last eight years. I used no medication, only herbal teas and similar holistic medicine during my pregnancy. I took raspberry tea regularly and drank protein supplements. I drank tea that strengthened the uterine wall and exercised. I encouraged my baby's development with imagery techniques in which you visualize your baby and mentally concentrate on aiding his growth. There are incredible photographs available that aid visualization immensely.

I went to a holistic clinic in Arizona two weeks before my child was due. I wanted Dr. Gladys McGeary of the clinic to deliver my baby. My husband Henry arrived from Los Angeles in time to take the baby out with his hands and cut the cord. I was in labor for twenty-four hours and the actual pushing took two. I remember asking Gladys, "What happens if I can't make it through?" She laughed and said, "Everybody asks that question. Believe me, you'll make it."

Dorian nursed until recently. I ate like a horse to keep up my strength and when he began to cut back suckling I couldn't figure out why I was gaining weight. By the time he was two and a half, he nursed morning and night. We talked one day and I said, "We're going to end this in two weeks so you'll have to prepare yourself." For the first week, he nursed at night. For the second week, he nursed every other night. We talked about the coming last night. He never cried about stopping.

When I am on location, we use a motor home as a base away from home. It's a small, mobile apartment. Dorian is in nursery school, and during productions, he will go for a half day and then come to the motor home. When I finish a shot, I retreat to home base. At night, we drive home to bed. I am always in contact with him no matter what the location. I always have the chance to kiss him good night.

The shooting of *I Want to Live* ended with my character's death in the gas chamber. Every day, I told Dorian that I was going to work and I'd describe for him the scenes we'd do that day. I didn't talk to him about the death scene. I was nervous, I suppose, even though we had already filmed many scenes in which I was hysterical or screaming and Dorian had never been upset.

We did the scene in one take and at the cut my secretary was standing at the edge of the set saying, "Lindsay, get back to the home quick! Dorian is crying and we can't get him to stop!" Dorian never cried, except for hunger. I ran to the motor home and picked Dorian up. He looked into my eyes and clung hard. He had started to sob two minutes before my secretary had come to get me. When he began to cry, my character was dying. This may have been a terrible coincidence. He may have had gas pains. I prefer to believe that it's evidence of the wonderful link between a mother and her child.

# TAMMY GRIMES
· · · ·

*Tammy Grimes was discovered by Noël Coward when she appeared in a New York City cabaret. He then cast her in her first Broadway play,* Lulu, *which launched her theatrical career. She went on to win Tony awards for her roles in* The Unsinkable Molly Brown *and* Private Lives. *She has starred in her own television series* The Tammy Grimes Show. *It has been said that her recorded voice is the most famous woman's voice in America. Tammy was twice awarded the Mother of the Year Award. She and her daughter Amanda Plummer, the actress, live in New York City.*

When I was a teenager, I wanted to be a star with a wonderful husband and four children by the age of twenty. When I was twenty-four, I'd married my knight in shining armor, Christopher Plummer, and had our daughter Amanda.

I was starring in a Broadway show called *The Unsinkable Molly Brown.* My wishes had all come true. By the time you're thirty, if you think you have realized all your dreams, you think you're an old lady and there's not much left. Amanda is the only thing that's lasted in my life. My marriages didn't last. I suppose my work has lasted, but apart from my parents and siblings, Amanda is the only person I deeply love.

I could almost tell she'd grown. Something would be different, and I could never quite catch up with the changes. She was always a surprise, always fascinating. I wanted to hang on to that special love, that deep feeling accompanied by pain. I never wanted Amanda to grow up. I missed her dreadfully. The times we spent together took on a special intimacy, a quality that I remember best from the day I woke up and my daughter was brought to me in the hospital. I won't top that feeling in my lifetime.

Amanda took it for granted that all mothers had the same routine I did. In school she realized other mothers were not the same. I could never have been happy giving up my work and Amanda would inevitably have felt guilty. Mothers have to tell themselves that they mustn't feel guilty about anything. We can't compare ourselves to the unattainable perfection of imaginary parents. Amanda's childhood was filled with nannies. Swedish nannies, German nannies, French nannies, Scottish nannies, and Irish nannies. We once had a German nanny who accompanied us on the road for *Molly Brown*. One day, I found the source of the strange smell that had followed us around for days. Amanda had been washing a huge doll she carried with her and it was waterlogged. Our luggage was enormously heavy and it wasn't just the doll; the nanny had also packed her health food—tin cans, fruit, jars upon jars. We were dragging a store around America. I tell Amanda she should write a book, but, of course, she saw it all quite differently.

Amanda watched me from backstage at the age of two. Sometimes on Sunday matinees, I'd bring her on stage if I could, hidden underneath my coat. I always told her she had to keep very quiet and as the kids in the stage chorus trooped by, she'd whisper, "Shhhh!"

I used to dream that Amanda would marry a wonderful man who

bred racehorses in Kentucky and I'd sit by the fire with my
grandchildren. Instead, Amanda has followed me into this
business. I said, "After all these years living with me, how could
you possibly want to act?" We agreed she'd go to Middlebury
College, and in her third year she called up and said, "My mind
is white. The walls are white, the mountains are white, and I've
got to go."

We've supported each other's career ever since. When I went to
see the opening of *Agnes of God,* I was tremendously thrilled and
tremendously critical. Fortunately, she can take it. Amanda is
very tactful about my performances. She'll say, "That was
beautiful. Better than the last, much better than the last."

When she was fifteen, I shipped her to Ireland to learn how to
hunt. She cried on the way to the airport. I said, "Amanda, you
love horses. If you can't stand it, come back in two weeks." She
returned the day school started. I could only reach her by mail. I
couldn't even telegraph her. During college, I put her on a plane
to Egypt with the family of one of her friends. Driving back from
the airport, I suddenly thought, "I just sent my daughter to
Egypt? Wait a minute—" I was learning how hard it was to walk
away.

47

# JUDY LICHT

*Judy Licht has long been a part of New York City journalism. In television*

*she has anchored noon and evening newscasts, hosted a morning talk show,*

*and reported for ABC, CBS, and Metromedia. She and her husband,*

*adman Jerry Della Femina, have a daughter, Jesse.*

For the first time in my life I've put my career in a secondary position. Previously, I had put it ahead of my marriage and my personal life; ahead of everything. I never had a balanced family life, not since I was eighteen years old. At forty, I finally have a family to come home to. The ordinary to me is impossibly exotic and delicious, a wonderful case of delayed gratification. Maybe I'll be bored in a year and go back and work hard, but for now I'm caught up.

I've just realized a lifelong dream—a work week unheard of in reporting. I work hard for three days and then I have four days to spend with my family. After my news show was canceled by new management, I received an offer from a competing station to anchor a wonderful program. It meant working seven days a week on live television doing something I had always wanted to do. I thought hard for two weeks and finally went back to my boss and said, "I'll report three days a week because I want to spend time with my family." I surprised everyone by sticking with my old station and the reduced work time. I love my work now because it's just the time I want to spend.

Every woman I know has said that my baby Jesse has been lucky for me. Since I no longer struggle to prove myself, I feel secure. I work more efficiently; I put in less effort for the same result. As a mother, your priorities change because you're burdened with less angst, less anger. I'm content simply because I can walk with Jesse and point out an airplane in the sky. The wonderment on her face is far greater than the audience's reaction to the best piece of journalism I'll ever produce.

Until the last months of my pregnancy, I worked seven-hour days.

I had an inordinate amount of energy. When I was tired, I'd drift into the ladies' room and lie down on a ratty old couch. I grew enormous; my old boss said I looked like the front end of a Buick. I was never morning sick.

Labor was very difficult. It went on for three days. I was exhausted. They had given me Pitocin and it really did intensify the pain. I was pushing damned hard and the doctor wasn't impressed. He finally determined the baby was in an odd position and would have to be delivered by forceps. I asked for an epidural and it took on just one side. A maternity nurse made the staff come back and complete the job. Maternity nurses are heroes, the ombudsmen of the delivery room.

I went back to work early and worked eight or nine hours a day, five days a week, on a new show, *First Edition News.* People were telling me, "A new show and a baby! You have such a wonderful life." I was repressing my anger because I wasn't with Jesse. At six months, babies suddenly develop a personality and if you're not there you miss them terribly. You've fallen in love. If I was at the station past three, I'd begin to snarl. Jerry suffered too. Every couple seems to have a rough time those first three months. Several weeks later, I went to the three-days-a-week schedule. The new show had been canceled. Their timing was perfect.

I postponed a lot of gratification in my life because I wanted to succeed. When I was twenty-five, I had a tremendous biological urge to have children, but I would have been too tied down. Later, I wanted a husband, a home, and children. It was not all fun being alone all those years, living in a studio apartment and not knowing if I could afford what I was spending and having to work long hours. You are jealous when you see friends your age with husbands, kids, and big houses, enjoying the security that brings. Now, in the end, I have those things. You have to create your own life before you have children and that takes delay and sacrifice. There's no free lunch anywhere along the road.

50

S U S A N  R O T H E N B E R G
. . . .

*Susan Rothenberg had the first exhibition of her painting in 1975. In the decade since she has established herself as one of the most successful and influential painters of her generation. Her work can be seen in such major collections as the Museum of Modern Art and the Whitney Museum of American Art. She gave birth to her daughter Maggie in 1972.*

When I told my mother I was pregnant, she said, "Oh no!" I never gave my mother any reason to think that I was responsible and could raise a child. I had always just gone off and done things. In my junior year, I left college and took a passenger liner to Greece. I couldn't balance a checkbook. I didn't dress well. I was married to a sculptor who drove a 1964 Dodge truck that he still has and whose clothing consisted of a red-and-black lumber jacket and a black T-shirt. Mother thought we were two artists living a funky life with no amenities and how could we bring a child into that situation?

I had never thought about having a child. A doctor once told me after a gynecological exam that it was unlikely I'd ever conceive. A year later, I went back and got on the table and I was pregnant. My body had done something inconceivable. I had lucked out.

The baby ultimately led to my success. If there was no baby there would be no work. I didn't understand working because I didn't understand work hours. Prior to her birth I was certainly in New York painting, but I was also going to movies, going to parties, meeting people. It was a time when all kinds of painters, musicians, and dancers were dining together, interacting, attending rehearsals of each other's work. Steve Reich, Philip Glass, Patricia Burns—all the artists were very interwoven. Maggie ended the visits for me. I had to be home with her, and I suffered a bit of an identity crisis about being someone's wife and someone's mother. I now wanted to create something and use my time well if I was stuck at home all day.

My husband built a part of the loft into a very large play area about twenty feet square that was fenced in and baby-proofed. I painted, and while I painted, I sang or tossed toys to her. She was right in the room with me and she could see me and hear the music. I tried to keep her in the corral as long as possible because of nails and staples on the floor.

I worked on patterns and abstract work, and in 1974, when Maggie was two, I started the horse paintings that were in my first show. I changed to watercolors so I could wash my hands to nurse her or change the diapers or whatever needed to be done. I have some great pictures of Maggie and me in a total mess.

George is a site sculptor and he was gone most of the time. I couldn't cope. There were fairly simple things to be done that I could handle, but then it would be winter and George would stay up all night, shoveling coal into the stove we used for heat. During the winter months, Maggie was constantly colicky. We only knew one other couple who had a child at the time and we didn't know anyone who would baby-sit. It was hard, isolated, and we were very different because we had a child. We took her everywhere, to concerts and wherever we could, but we dropped out of social activities.

I withdrew more than I needed to. People might have been more
amenable if I had known how to trust. Instead, I took my
motherhood very seriously. When my mother-in-law came to visit
and wanted to hold Maggie, we pulled the child in opposite
directions. I became terrified if I was out of the house and caught
in a traffic jam.

I had never heard that a mother couldn't paint and I was
determined to try. Everybody's different. Elizabeth Murray is a
wonderful mother and painter who has always painted with babies
around her, with help, without help. Lois Lane Kemp can't paint
if she hears her baby's voice in another room. Today, I can't have
Maggie in the studio. I try to be patient, but I can't have the
questions and interruptions.

When Maggie was young, I painted while she was awake. I was
lucky. I wrapped my head around my work and the process
became smoother and smoother. Finally, she went to school. I had
four or five hours a day and time after she was in bed. I
occasionally snuck back in my studio at ten o'clock and painted
all night.

55
. . . .

My output has been incredibly even for the last ten or twelve years. I usually do between ten and fifteen paintings a year and I think it'll stay that way. I'm not a prolific artist because my days are so dispersed. I overwork one painting rather than produce many. I'd rather attempt to fix the canvas than try to get it right the next time. It's just the nature of how I handle problems. Maggie has not affected my productivity. I count my serious painting from her birth, from the end of haphazardness.

Maggie was five or six when George and I parted and the divorce definitely took a toll on her. She has had to divide her heart in half. George and I each have equal shares and she feels very loved by both of us. We spend her birthday and Christmases together, not pretending to be a family, but still together. Each time she's mad at me, she wants to leave, and it was a relief to find that she says the same things in the other house. We let her make the phone call and the other parent will say, "No, you can't come over right now."

If I could do it over, I guess I'd be more patient and not have gotten a divorce. It would have been much better for her to grow up with her father and I'm sorry our separation happened.

Maggie is a little woman now. She's sensitive, noisy, and easily moved to tears. She never laughs on cue. Her responses are deeper than mine, and she's lovable, with a tremendous amount of love inside of her. She's very comfortable with adults.

Lately she's been saying, "I think I'd like to be famous also." I reply, "What do you want that for? You think I like that nonsense?" But she enjoys it. She gets a charge out of people coming up to me.

I tell her to like the work you spend your life doing. Pick a challenging career. Beyond that, I don't choose to give her any direction about how she should live. I'll be content to be a shoulder for her to cry on as she gets older, just as my mother did for me.

# R A E  D A W N  C H O N G
· · · ·

*Rae Dawn Chong is the daughter of Tommy Chong of the comedy team "Cheech and Chong." She grew up in Vancouver and Los Angeles. In sixth grade she was discovered by a Walt Disney talent scout. After attracting notice in Alan Rudolph's film* Choosing You, *she starred in 1982's* Quest for Fire. *Her career has since included* Commando *and* The Color Purple. *She gave birth to her son Morgan when she was twenty-one.*

My pregnancy was not well thought out. However, I was ready to take the time and make the sacrifices a child requires. There weren't any parties to miss, places to see, people to meet, that were more important than having a child. Biologically, it was no longer Rae Dawn Chong; it was Rae Dawn Chong and child.

The trials started with my weight. I gained sixty pounds, and made an appearance on *Good Morning America* as Rae Dawn Chong, the beached whale. I had to tell myself that I didn't live for the industry, and if motherhood meant a broader-hipped body, well, there have been tougher sacrifices.

After Morgan was born, I went back to work. I'd like to tell the career-minded woman: Remember lazily looking around for your shoulder pads? Taking half an hour for makeup? Bringing home that cute date? You'd better sit back, relax, and adjust. Makeup's ten minutes. If you do get to sleep, it's alone, and no sleeping in.

I'm hit hardest by guilt. I do want to be that Betty Crocker mom. I want to bake cookies and always be home. Morgan is very bright, so he understands my guilt and plays off it. Guilt is a destructive emotion and I hurt Morgan by not being decisive. When I realized that, I told him, "Forget it, kid, you aren't going to manipulate me. Momma's going to work because those toys you love so much come from what I do." By not bending I demonstrate inner strength. By demanding respect for my identity as a mother and a professional, I set an example. Morgan is going to grow up strong and secure. He's going to believe in himself. I

truly believe that I've given him a great gift by showing him I am a mother and an actress.

I treat my son as an individual. In return, he doesn't lie to me; he tells me everything. I'm sure we'll always be that close. I do worry like every mother, though. One of the problems of how we raise our children is that when they're around twelve to sixteen, we lose touch. We don't know who they are. If I sense I don't know Morgan anymore, I will stop my life, turn to him, and say, "Let's go to Africa and get reacquainted." I wish I'd heard that from my mom and dad, because they lost me for a few years. Only recently have we become friends again. Kids kill themselves because they're alone, and it's not because they aren't loved; it's because their parents are too busy to notice the stranger in the house.

I discipline Morgan, but I don't try to manipulate him; I let him be. I especially don't want to punish Morgan by letting him know he's smaller and weaker than I am. Spanking violates a child's identity and sense of free choice. It's demeaning. With Morgan, I'll say, "Go upstairs, close the door, and talk to me when you want to be nice." I never liked spanking; it didn't work, and I didn't respect my parents for it.

Since I do want to continue as an actress, I have to plan carefully how work merges with family. Before Morgan, I had an apartment. I could go wherever I wanted. Now I have a staff and I just bought a house to put the staff in! This year will be big again—maybe two or three films—so we'll be on the road with all the decisions that entails. I take Morgan with me if I'm gone over a week, otherwise he freaks out. He really misses me.

Thankfully, we love it on location. Since I have a son, the crew doesn't work me past nine-thirty. Morgan behaves himself despite the distractions of the set. Hollywood poses special problems. I no longer let him on the set after he walked in on a scene for the movie *Commando.* In the scene, someone is murdered and, unfortunately, I was too busy to say, "Get him out!" Morgan heard the shots, saw the action, and connected it with *He-man, Roadrunner,* and other violent cartoons, so naturally he was scared for his mom. I had to look over and say, "It's only make-believe. We're just pretending."

I am a single parent. I don't know if I feel comfortable being independent since my instinct is to be hugged, nurtured, and taken care of. I'm still missing that perfect relationship. I don't know many men who will tolerate an opinionated woman with youth, success, a career; someone who's independent, loves sex, jewels, and travel. So I stay free. I'm never far from available, wonderful men, but those flowers in the field stay unplucked. It's better that way for Morgan, too.

I had an immature notion of beauty as perfection. After the birth my stretch-marked body didn't mesh with that. It took a year to get back in shape, but right now I feel fabulous, very sexy. Being a mother has made me appreciate being a woman more. I've strengthened my ties to my own mother, too, and to my stepmother, magnificent women, both. All that feminine energy! I feel quite wealthy.

I think back to an evening when Morgan was four months old. I had split up with his father, and I was twenty pounds overweight. Morgan squirmed under my arms as I made dinner. The phone rang and my agent told me I was rejected for a part. The laundry wasn't done upstairs. I began to cry about my life. I must have tickled Morgan because he started to giggle and laugh. I suddenly felt that I could go on and do anything.

# J U D Y   W O O D R U F F

*Judy Woodruff is the chief Washington correspondent for* The MacNeil/
Lehrer Newshour. *She also anchors her own PBS documentary series,*
Frontline. *From 1977 to 1982 she served as the White House
correspondent, covering both the Carter and Reagan administrations, for
NBC. In 1982 she joined* The Today Show *as their Washington reporter.
She is married to Albert Hunt, Washington Bureau chief of* The Wall
Street Journal, *and they have a son Jeffrey.*

When Jeffrey was two months old, the President bounced him
on his knee. I had brought Jeffrey to visit the White House
reporters and friends on the White House staff. The staff arranged
for the President to see me and they secretly invited my husband.
I had just finished feeding Jeffrey and I was about to burp him
when someone said, "The President can see you now."

We walked into the Oval Office and the President immediately
asked to hold Jeffrey. Al and I hoped Jeffrey wouldn't make a
mess of the President's suit. Ronald Reagan had a meeting with
the President of Sudan next, and I couldn't see him walking in
with a diaper held to his shoulder. He sang a nursery rhyme to
Jeffrey, "This is the way the ladies ride, this is the way the
gentlemen ride, this is the way the cowboys ride—" while
bouncing Jeffrey on his knee. The bouncing made me nervous.
Would he spit up?

I took three and a half months of leave from covering the White
House. It's a very demanding job—despite the perks of visiting
the President—because you're continually at the beck and call of
the White House press office. I needed those months to get used
to having another human being around. I thought my life had
been nicely organized and compartmentalized, but when I looked
in the evening at the list of daily tasks I'd prepared in the
morning, I'd found that I hadn't done any of them. Nursing,
worrying, and telephoning had become a full-time occupation.

The hardest adjustment was realizing how little personal time was left for me. Now that I have a child, the day is work, child, and husband. Al spends all the time with Jeffrey he can and fills in for me when necessary. He once took Jeffrey with him on an assignment out West when I had to fill in for Jane Pauley on *The Today Show*. A father on the road with a baby is a special rarity who receives lots of attention and help, but Al still came back utterly exhausted. For me, the pendulum swings. There are days when I effortlessly combine motherhood and career and there are times when I'm a crumpled heap thinking, "I can't go on." Fortunately, those moments pass and you go on to the next step.

Female journalists with children are still an exception. Anne Compton has four children and covers Congress for ABC. I admire her tremendously. Her husband's a doctor, she has a full-time job, and somehow she handles four children. Jane Pauley gets up at one or two in the morning, but she calibrates her day to leave her with a block of time with the kids in the afternoon or the evening. At CBS, Lesley Stahl has a daughter in school. They apparently made a decision to have just one child. There are others, but the norm is to stay single.

I always felt there would be time for children. I didn't want to get married early; I married at the age of thirty-three and I had Jeffrey a year later. I have friends in their thirties who come to me and say, "My life is too fixed for children." I wonder how that compares with the added dimensions of life that come with having a child, but I respect their decision. I'd be miserable if I couldn't continue in my career. I hope the smart employer realizes that women with children will trade an extra ounce of dedication for not having to stay those additional evenings. They work because they love their career or because they need to provide for their family. Hopefully, more employers realize this, but we don't have any real evidence. There's been no massive corporate shift in this country toward underwriting or supporting the kind of elaborate child-care that's found in Europe.

I'm certainly interested in issues like childcare, but the story I love to cover is politics, and most of politics doesn't relate to women's issues. I'm not able to incorporate many of my personal interests into our stories, but we occasionally run a story on child-care or maternity leave. I don't think reporters should crusade for their personal interests. You've got to try and keep some semblance of an open mind.

With Jeffrey, I never had any problems and I ran around until the last minute. With my second pregnancy, I'm trying to relax; I don't want to overexert myself and land flat on my back for two days. My doctor wants me to stop traveling and I need to cover several Senate races so I'm walking a fine line. I probably won't take as much maternity leave this time around.

Al and I usually share duties with Jeffrey. We divide the job of getting him ready to go to school in the morning; one of us gets him up while the other makes breakfast, and the other one dresses him and so forth. In the evening we take turns at reading him a story and it's lights out at eight-thirty. We try to save week nights for him, and during the summer we're all together at a small house we bought in the Chesapeakes from Friday evening to Sunday. Al and Jeffrey play with the motorboat and go crabbing. Other times, weekends are like they are everywhere—errands, soccer games, and church on Sundays. We have to work at it, though. One year, Al and I would wake up on Saturday, examine our lists of errands, and trade Jeffrey back and forth during the day as we rushed about getting things done. We weren't together at all. The struggle never lets up.

67

*After graduating from Brandeis University, Joyce Chopra studied acting*
*and then opened a folk music coffeehouse, featuring the then-unknown Joan*
*Baez. After one of her first films,* A Happy Mother's Day, *won a Bronze*
*Medal at the Venice Film Festival, she went on to produce and direct many*
*award-winning documentaries, including* Joyce at 34, Martha Clarke Light
and Dark: A Dancer's Journal, *and* Music Lessons. *She recently released*
*her first full-length dramatic film, the critically acclaimed* Smooth Talk.
*She produced her husband Tom Cole's Vietnam play* Medal of Honor Rag
*for American Playhouse and they collaborated on the play* The Woman
Warrior. *They have a daughter, Sarah.*

In 1971 my mother exclaimed in my film *Joyce at 34,* "I couldn't believe that at her age she was nursing a baby." I was thirty-four. *Joyce at 34* was a documentary about my pregnancy and the first year of life of my child; it is also witness to how our attitudes toward working women and family have changed since the beginning of the seventies.

A sociologist friend of mine from Harvard asked me to make that film. She said, "You're in a unique position to do a film about yourself, your child, and your mother." I thought, "God, how narcissistic," but my mind kept churning out scenes. I ended up with a film about the conflicts of parenting and work. *Joyce at 34* begins with Sarah's birth and ends with her first steps, but there is no plot and no conclusion, just a look at the troubles of the first year.

Today, I'd add a cautionary note to any working woman watching Joyce in the film. Do not do what I did! I was desperate to demonstrate that a baby wouldn't affect my life at all. I toted her everywhere. I kept working. I breast-fed her until her sixth month. I had people running after me with the baby. It was insanity and if I had a baby now I wouldn't dream of killing myself that way.

The best insight I received during this period came from my husband's mother. We drove up one weekend and unloaded the car. Out came the portable crib, the infant seat, the bags of Pampers, all the paraphernalia of the liberated, mobile couple. Tom's mother watched and finally she remarked, "We didn't have any of this equipment when I had my kids. I couldn't go anywhere for a year. I was lucky. You have the illusion your life hasn't changed."

In 1972 none of my friends were even having children. Claudia Weill, my coproducer on *Joyce at 34*, did a film that year on every woman's vision of what having a baby would be like; the child cries and cries and utterly wrecks her mother's career as a photographer. Those of us with babies were determined to demonstrate that we could go on with our lives.

If I see a change in attitude over a decade, it may be as a result of my experience as a free-lance worker who sets her own hours. I know I'd never work again the way I did in 1972. Certainly, it's easier for older women to have children. Claudia recently had

a child. She's thirty-nine or forty and she's never been happier. A friend of mine wants a baby but she's the head of a large corporate division. If she takes time off for her child, she's going to be swept away. What makes the eighties different for her? A year off is still very dangerous.

A French art historian has a theory that childhood as a time apart is an invention of the nineteenth century when families stopped working together and we had a breakdown of culture. If you look at paintings prior to this, everyone is dressed in the same way. Grown-ups play games with children in village scenes and children worked at the age of twelve. Today, we have a separation of work and family that makes it much harder to merge the two. Sarah has grown up in an unusual way for our time; she is a part of my career.

From very early on, I took her to all my meetings. I would go to an office and walk in on people I didn't know and introduce them to my daughter. She sat around in a lot of restaurants, reading a book. She adapted well. She knows enough about making movies

71
. . . . .

and writing to be the head of a studio as far as I'm concerned. Today, I have her read scripts I'm interested in because I value her opinion on whether a script will work.

For *Smooth Talk,* Sarah was a sounding board and procurer of scenes. She came home from school with snippets of dialogue from her friends. A lot of the hanging around and Mall scenes are Sarah's contribution. For example, there's a scene in which the girls are standing in line for a movie theater and one of them complains that her mother is a religious fanatic and she wants her daughter to start attending Mass. Sarah heard that in a girls' room one morning. We began listening to contemporary music to find a soundtrack for *Smooth Talk.* I was out of touch and Sarah was just starting to be interested in what was on the radio. It was wonderful. We bought tapes and listened to them, and I eventually wound up with James Taylor.

As an adolescent, Sarah contributed to the film by just tuning me in to what girls that age are feeling. In the film, the girls describe junior high and one of them said, "Well, they were always so awful to you in the past, but now the boys are so nice to you." I gave Connie, the main character, that line, "The boys are so nice . . . ." The other day, Sarah murmured it, and then realized what she was saying. That line breaks my heart.

I feel very fortunate in not having the separation between work and family that most working women take for granted. Claudia and I interviewed a group of retired women in Brooklyn for *Joyce at 34.* The scene starts with the women showing each other pictures of their children, their grandchildren. They oh and ah. Finally I ask them one question, "Did you have any conflicts about working and mothering?" Explosion! They couldn't stop talking. The scene ends with a New York Jewish mother declaring, "If I stay home I'm bored and that's not good for him. If I go to work I come home tired and that's not good for me. Whatever we do is wrong." It was the early seventies, and she had received her first chance to talk about what was wrong with working and being a mother. It was a very exciting time.

73

# CARLY SIMON
· · · ·

*Carly Simon is the third daughter of Richard Simon, the cofounder of Simon & Schuster. Her solo career began in 1971 with the album* That's the Way I've Always Heard It Should Be *and a Grammy Award as Best New Artist. The hit 1972 single "You're So Vain" launched her into an award-studded, thirteen-album career as one of the top female vocalists of the seventies and eighties. In 1972, she married singer/songwriter James Taylor. They have two children from their eleven-year marriage, Sarah and Ben.*

There was a great line in the film *Heartburn,* for which I wrote the score. The wife says to her therapist, "If the marriage doesn't work out, I can get a divorce." The therapist replies, "Well, you know, divorce is only a temporary solution." In other words, you can divorce, but you can't unmarry.

The first week James and I lived together, we named our children-to-be. The girl would be Sarah and the boy would be Ben. Sarah came first. Fortunately, my work has a kind of floating nature to it, and I took off five or six months after Sarah was born. I was still working, even if I wasn't putting pen to paper. I write in my head and construct songs before I actually put them down. During the five months I spent nursing her, I wrote songs. A lot of the rock 'n' roll tunes on my albums began in the nursery. "Terra Nova" started out as the musical accompaniment to one of Sarah's toys. It's now a song on James's album *J.T.* Singing to the children inspired me and I am still influenced by their tastes.

I breast-fed Ben until he was three years old. He began to nurse even before the umbilical cord was cut. Skeptical friends called me "The Milkman," but the physical bonding and the sheer nourishment of mother's milk gave my three-year-old son the resources to overcome a major operation. One of his kidneys was malformed: It leaked toxins into his bloodstream. Ben was very,

very ill until he was old enough to undergo surgery. The bond between us kept him going. Where else is love that pure?

I don't know if I could go through an experience like that again —I felt so helpless and scared. It's one of the things that stops me when I think of having another child. My family—and especially my sister Lucy—got me through those years. Today Ben is a really happy and healthy kid, even though he can't play football.

Ben was ill while my marriage to James was breaking up. I was overwhelmed by stress and fear and I had no one in my life to share my problems with. Eventually the children and I adjusted, but the divorce has brought with it a whole new set of problems for them. Ben tells me he misses Dad when he's with me, and he misses me when he's with Dad. There's never a time when he doesn't miss the love of one of us; there's never a time when he can have the love of both parents together.

As long as you have a family, your children are your bond to the other parent. Unless that connection is amicable, your children face terrible pain and trouble. It's supposedly much better if the parents are divorced rather than living together and always fighting, but what if they're divorced and still not getting along? Then both parents aren't even around at the same time. The periods I have with James in which we don't handle matters amicably are filled with pain and stress and often there isn't a great deal of opportunity to smooth the waters, to work together for Sarah and Ben. But James is a loving father, and he calls them from on the road; I'd say he's better than 80 percent of the fathers I know.

When the children are with me, I am with them. Because I am divorced, I want to give them more to fill this awful lack, this awful thing that happened to them. I want to make it up to them in time and in quality. It's not guilt; I am not acting out of guilt, but, rather, when I'm with my children, I don't want to leave. If I can't take them out of school to be with me on a project, I simply don't go. I'll turn down film roles; I'll turn down anything. It's a rule, and the refusal's easy.

I'm able to continue recording, since it fits in with my schedule. Sometimes I may not be with the kids when they come home from school, but I never record over the weekend so my time is theirs. I haven't really toured since either of the kids was born; I was on the road just once with Sarah before she was school-age.

My children come first and perhaps I spoil them, although not with possessions. I picked them up every time they cried and I still dote on them. I was never the kind of mother who thought that the children should be left alone to cry. If they ask for love or cuddling, I'll definitely be there for all they need.

Both my children are very aware aurally and visually and they have a wonderful sense of style. From the time the babies were very small, I always wore bangles and great-colored earrings that they could look at. There were bright and colorful objects in their rooms, and I'd point out a sunset, a house, a color. I've tried to stimulate their senses in all ways.

I learned this and so much more from my mother. I always sang to my children because she sang to me. I've found that I've become my mother more and more, that I've been lucky to have had such a fascinating woman raise me. Hopefully, we can pick and choose the good qualities of our mothers—the parts of their personalities that made us happy—and disassociate ourselves from the rest. She's still alive and she passes on to me her drama, her excitement, and her zestful appreciation of life.

Motherhood has been the most joyous and important experience of my life. I would die for my children.

# S U S A N  F I S H E R

. . . .

*As a senior vice president at Manufacturers and Traders Trust Company,*

*Susan Fisher is responsible for providing banking services to many of the*

*world's wealthiest individuals. In her previous tenure at Marine Midland*

*Bank, she created a highly profitable Private Banking Department which*

*in its first year attracted six hundred customers and $200 million in assets.*

*Susan is a board member of many organizations and serves as the national*

*chairman of the Republican's Woman Coalition. She and her husband, Dr.*

*Yale Fisher, prominent eye surgeon, have two children, Douglas and Robin.*

I have a high-energy lifestyle, but it's always been that way for me. I never considered not having a family simply because I was busy. Yale and I were married when I was twenty-one, and I thought about a child three years later when Yale was in the Army, but he was sent to Fort Monmouth in New Jersey, a very long commute to New York. We went back and forth, and talked about a baby in the future. There was no rush.

I decided that before having children I would try to reach a level of seniority where my company would know I was serious about my career. When I was twenty-eight, I had an early miscarriage, the sort that unfortunately happens to even the healthiest women. Soon after, I went to business school. I did my homework between midnight and four in the morning, and in my final semester I became pregnant. I was enrolled at Columbia, working full-time, pregnant, and my bank decided to send me to a two-week program at Harvard. It was crazy. I eventually delivered early and finished my classes on time. I nursed Doug for six months during this. My bank was astounded to discover that not only had I enrolled in business school while working, but I was months pregnant as well. They eventually left me alone for four or five months and avoided assigning me extra duties. Doug slept four or five hours at a stretch, and I found cab services that would bring me home during the day for his feeding. Neither Doug nor Robin ever tasted formula. I love the closeness of nursing, and Robin never had more than eight to ten bottles in eight months of nursing.

I'm now at a level of seniority where a family is easier than if I were lower-ranked and trying to "do it all." When you run your division, you set the time of the meetings. You've learned through experience what works and what doesn't. I've tried very hard to fit my meetings within the nine-to-five day even though much of my business is breakfast, lunch, and dinner. Breakfast may now be croissants in the office at nine-thirty. Drinks will be at five o'clock instead of seven. Fortunately, business has come a long way in understanding the time pressure that results from the obligations of family. Still, if my boss wants me at the corporate headquarters in Buffalo, I'll be there.

During the week, I always try to be home for a few hours in the evening. Often, I stay in until nine-thirty; I put Robin to bed and help Doug with his homework, and then I'll slip away to have a drink with a client who's already been taken out to dinner by an associate. At busy times, I work to balance extra hours with my children's needs. The other night, for example, Doug needed help with an essay. He called at five-twenty, just before a board meeting, and I coached him for ten minutes over the phone. When I got home, it was almost his bedtime, but we worked together correcting the grammar for an hour. I've learned to slide those minutes in.

There are times when my children have responded to my schedule less well than others. The beauty about children is that they *tell* you. Douglas told me he wanted to be a doctor and not a business person because my husband often gets home at four-thirty in the afternoon when he does surgery. I can never do that. Douglas said he did not want to be a business person because they don't have enough time with their families and he was obviously looking at me. In the past year he has seen a big change in my schedule and we spend more time together.

I take my children away alone once or twice a year just to be with them and I find that tremendously valuable. Most of my business is in New York, but I do a fair amount of public speaking, so I have a minimum of eight or ten business trips a year.

From Saturday morning to Sunday night, I'm with the children; absolutely no weddings or bar mitzvahs. I bicycle with Doug in Central Park and we go to museums or visit friends in the country. I love to take Doug and Robin to the South Street Seaport. I travel less on business than I used to, but I still need to be away occasionally. I don't like being away from the children, and the mail builds up; the office sends home correspondence even if I've been gone one night.

I need just three or four hours of sleep each night. I treasure the extra hours for reading because I need those night hours of free time to visit friends. Exercise is a daily necessity; I have so much energy I don't think about stress, but it's inevitable given my job. In the morning I wake, stretch, lift weights, and ride my exercise bike for twenty minutes while scanning the paper. If I'm getting my hair done, the hairdresser arrives, and afterwards I go to work.

I broke all the rules when I had my children. I was out only a week each time. I was so excited about my work I came right back. The president of the bank told me that I had the energy of two people and he used to repeat that in training programs. I love my career. Of course, it's easier with newborns because they sleep so much. They're much easier to say good-bye to than two-year-olds.

I find that I've sacrificed very little because I'm blessed with a ridiculous amount of energy. Yale and I haven't always had the time together we'd like and I miss not seeing my friends as often as I'd wish. I like to think, though, that as I recognized a gap in my life I changed my priorities and rearranged my life according to what's important. As your children grow, their needs change, and I hope I'm there adapting alongside them.

*Betsey Johnson was born in Wethersfield, Connecticut. She became a*
*sensation in the sixties designing "pop" clothes for the early youth*
*revolution. She received her first Coty Award in 1971. Betsey was thirty-*
*three and unmarried when she became pregnant. She has raised Lulu alone*
*for the past eleven years.*

I heard those chemical bells which say "kid time" when I was
thirty-three. I think having a kid is a separate thing from
anything else in your life. It is so much bigger than your career
or how much money you are making. It is that old-fashioned idea
of family that I definitely knew I wanted. I'm just one of those
women who thinks there should be sperm banks.

It was important for me to know that I was going to be financially
okay and that there was lots of work for me to do. During the
pregnancy I always thought in the back of my head that I could
take care of this kid on my own. No matter what, I was definitely
setting up a lot of work, a lot of money. I did not want to think
that this relationship wasn't going to work out, but I did want to
think that if something was going to happen, that I would be
really fine on my own.

When I was pregnant everything was so exciting and I felt so
alive. I knew the day Lulu was coming. I saw the doctor and he
told me I was going to have twins. Afterwards I had a morning
show to launch my children's wear collection at the 21 Club,
which I commentated. I had lunch at the Ginger Man, ran over to
the office for some final fittings, stopped off to look at another
line I was doing, and got home at six o'clock. Lulu was born at
7:30 P.M. in just ten contractions.

The birth was the miracle every mother knows. It was like a real
great earthquake and wasn't like I had learned in the Lamaze
class.

Shortly after Lulu's birth I split up with Clark, her father. I felt

very protective of my offspring and all I cared about was that
Lulu was safe and around someone who really loved her. I
realized Clark wasn't able to give me materialistically or
emotionally what I insisted on, and we needed to be separate
from him. He really despised being taken care of by a woman,
and I financed the two of us.

The surprise to me was that motherhood came so naturally. Lulu
slept right next to me in a tiny crib. I think it is important that
you feel each other, just absorption through the senses. I
remember how as a child I would die for thunder and lightning
just so I could creep into my mother's bed.

My parents were mortified that I didn't go down the aisle, and
they didn't tell anybody I was pregnant. I was the only woman in
the family to be divorced or have a child without being married.
They accepted it because they were proud of me and underneath
frightened that I hadn't met the right man.

86

After I had the baby I felt like I had come out of the grave. I
was out of the hospital in half a day and the president of Gant
was down to the loft and we were working. I remember being in a
roomful of men up at Gant when Lulu needed to be fed. At first
they felt uncomfortable and straightened their ties. After five
minutes they relaxed because I was a professional. I just felt very
comfortable with Lulu and she was the closest thing to me. Maybe
they felt she was an appendage!

Because I don't cook I nursed her for nine months. It was much
easier to breast-feed her.

In the tiny baby stage I think it is so important to be alone for
little chunks of time, so that you get a sense of yourself again
and what your child means to you. I took Lulu with me to Hong
Kong when I was nursing. Later I would leave her behind with
my parents. I felt like a separate woman alone in the hotel, doing
my work, and it gave Lulu the opportunity to build the
relationship with my parents.

As a baby Lulu understood when I said, "Give me a break." Her first words, in fact, were "Give me a break." The greatest part was when we walked down the street and she said, "Mummy, that's yours"—when she put the pieces together and said "that's Mummy's work"—all the fabric, all the late hours, all the running around. Unless she was there with me all the way it would not have hit her that this was what I was doing and that it was most important to me.

There is a nice natural stubborn energy in her that I have too. She doesn't want me to have boyfriends—any lovelife. I said, "I feel the same way about you—you will have the same deal as I have." She said, "You're nuts!" Lulu is now into her heavy boyfriend stage and the excitement is the realization that she can talk to boys!

I would love to have another child if I could believe that I was going to fall in love again, but I have lost my flighty optimism about that. I think my work and Lulu make my decision about men.

*Sally Quinn was for many years a political reporter for the Washington*
Post, *famous for her coverage of the social scene as well as national*
*politics. Quinn was also coanchor of the* CBS Morning News, *an*
*experience she chronicled in* We're Going to Make You a Star. *She lives in*
*Washington, D.C., with her son Quinn and her husband Ben Bradlee,*
*executive editor of the Washington* Post. *Her recent novel,* Regrets Only,
*was a national bestseller.*

I had told Ben I never wanted a baby and he was thrilled. He
already had three children by his first marriage and four
stepchildren from his second. Ben was finished as a parent; he
was going to travel and live a wonderful life unencumbered by
more children. Ben now feels betrayed.

At the time, I thought of nothing but Ben and writing for the
Washington *Post.* I was crazed by ambition, and I believed then
as I do now that you can't juggle a relationship, a career, and a
child with success. Something has to give.

My friend Nora Ephron married and broke our sacred pact to
have no children. Ben and I were in Miami en route to St.
Maarten and he told me, "Great news. Nora's pregnant." I felt so
betrayed, I got drunk and passed out in the plane's bathroom. I
was devastated, not because of Nora's news, but because it
sparked an inner confrontation. I did want a child. I went to a
therapist and two years later finally admitted to myself that I
wanted marriage and children.

I told my therapist, "I don't want to get married but I want Ben
to want to marry me." I had told her I was really angry at Ben
because he did not want to get married. She said, "I think he
senses that you don't and he doesn't think that you are a good
marriage bet. Do you want to get married?" "No," I said, "I
don't want to get married but I want him to want to marry me."
It took a long time for me to admit to her and to myself that I

wanted to get married. I finally went to Ben and said, "I want to get married." He said, "Oh, you want to get married. Okay!" It really did happen like that. Next I started agitating about babies.

Pregnancy became a physical obsession more overwhelming than sexual desire, hunger, thirst, pain, or joy. Everyone on the street was pregnant! They were all pushing strollers, and I would stop dead on the sidewalk and clutch myself. I had to have a child. No negotiating. Ben thought it was a whim. Pregnancy was "in," and I was acting fashionable. I could not explain my compulsion to him; no male is ever going to understand this female biological urge. I finally told him I would have a baby and if it wasn't his, it would be someone else's. I was prepared to walk out on the man I loved.

I became pregnant on my fortieth birthday. I took a leave of absence to write a novel. There was indeed life outside the Washington *Post*. It was a perfect, idyllic pregnancy.

92

A few days after Quinn was born, the doctor discovered he had a heart defect, a heart murmur. After a month, she sent us to a cardiologist at the Children's Hospital. Quinn had a large hole in his heart. They told us it would close, but we were to watch for heart failure. It would be insidiously subtle. One day Quinn was fussing; he wouldn't nurse, and when we realized something was wrong, we rushed him to the emergency room. He was in heart failure, and we watched as they connected up the IV's and machines.

Quinn is faced with many residual problems because the doctors had him on a heart/lung machine during surgery. He has a lot of scar tissue on his lungs, and he's constantly threatened by pneumonia. Whatever comes along, he gets it first, has it worse than anyone else, and has it longer.

My low point was the summer of '85. He developed a seizure disorder, and we couldn't control it for six months. One seizure lasted fifteen minutes. We didn't know if there was brain damage, and then we found he had a speech problem, a possible sign of retardation.

I was exhausted. Quinn was two, and he had spent his life in Washington's Children's Hospital. At one point they thought he had cystic fibrosis. Next they were testing for AIDS because his immune system was not functioning. The doctors thought he had a permanent hearing loss; we had to prepare for ear surgery. I would get up off the mat; then, pow, I'd be right back down again.

This wasn't what I had anticipated. I got to be a mother in spades because it distracted me from the rest of my life. I couldn't write; I could only sit in front of my typewriter and weep. I had no creativity.

My career was the first thing to go. From working full out and flying around the world on foreign assignments, I went to a life focused on my child and my husband, even though I still had exciting projects to accomplish. I had work to do, and that feeling was somewhere in the pit of my stomach or the core of my soul all the time that Quinn was sick.

My friends gave me support, flexibility. The baby nurse from the hospital stayed for a year and a half, sleeping in Quinn's room at night. I'm grateful, too, for the environment at the Children's Hospital. It made an enormous difference seeing the staffers in white, working for the children.

Through all this, Quinn has remained the jolliest soul. He loves to go to the doctor. When we have his blood tested, he sticks out his arm and laughs when the bubble of blood comes. He takes it all in his stride. I don't think he has realized yet that this is not how other kids' lives are. He just started in nursery school and is doing very well, although he can't talk as well as other children. He thinks that people who can't understand him are stupid. The speech therapist told me to say, "Mommy is so dumb," when I can't understand what he's saying.

The fears we had about brain damage were groundless; Quinn is really smart. He may have a correctable hearing problem that accounts for his speech, but he is always going to have problems, he will always be on medication. If he cuts himself, we put him immediately on antibiotics. Still, we're lucky. So many other children are worse off. Ten million children a year end up in the hospital or emergency room. I'm writing a series of children's books about hospitals and sick children for Quinn and all the others. There aren't any books out there that really speak to him. Part of the proceeds will go to the Children's Hospital.

You go along thinking that disasters occur to someone else, not to me. Today I'm more vulnerable. Whenever I hear about something awful happening to a child, I think why can't that happen here? I try very hard to find the good in Quinn's trouble. Maybe I wouldn't have been as close to him. I might have gone back to my writing and not stayed as involved with my son as I've been.

Today I'm more sympathetic to people and their problems. I have not become a Pollyanna, someone who can claim that God won't give you more than you can handle. I don't claim that God blessed us with a special child. I wanted a child who wouldn't be sick. I've hated every minute, and there hasn't been a day that I haven't wished that Quinn had been healthy and well and never had to go through this—he wasn't. There is nothing I can do except give him my best and make him as well as he can be.

I feel very optimistic about him. My interest in my career has resumed, and there are a lot of things I want to do that are very exciting. That feeling was there somewhere in the pit of my stomach or the core of my soul all the time Quinn was sick. I know just what I want to do and how I want to raise my child and what kind of mother I want to be. I can't work full time the way I did before and be the kind of mother I want to be. I would like to raise a child who is totally happy and confident. That is the greatest gift a woman can give her child: a sense of security and confidence, happiness and optimism.

A N D I E M A C D O W E L L

*On her first visit to New York from South Carolina in 1978, Andie*

*MacDowell was signed by the Elite model agency. She went to Paris and*

*quickly became an international success. Her biggest break was the famous*

*"Dot and Earl" commercial for Calvin Klein jeans. She went on to*

*starring roles in* Greystoke: The Legend of Tarzan *and* St. Elmo's Fire.

*Andie is presently the spokesperson for L'Oreal Cosmetics. She and her*

*husband, model Paul Qualley, have a baby son, Justin.*

We were in Fiji when I said to my sister, "Babs, I'm not getting my period." During the next week we flew in a small airplane from island to island and each day I waited for my period or just for a sign as to why I felt so different. I wasn't especially alarmed. Children were always more important to me than a career; I had told myself I'd have a child when I was twenty-seven, career or no career, and that's exactly what happened.

I loved being pregnant. I only gained five pounds, and I never had to worry about even a single inch on my waist. I swam three days a week; swimming is much more fun when you're pregnant because you float easily and you're accompanied by the little friend in your belly. The swimming kept me in good shape up until the final two weeks when I at last started feeling fat. I was very confident until a friend told me about her seventy-two hours of labor, I just looked incredulous, fully unaware that my own labor would last four days.

I began contractions on Monday night. I took a shower twice and felt better, slept on and off, and went to my doctor in the morning. He saw I was having contractions and thought I'd probably go to the hospital that night. I arrived at the hospital at 3 A.M. Wednesday morning. The staff made me walk up and down the halls. I continued to have contractions. My husband sat in a wheelchair and watched. We looked as though we'd been on a drinking binge for days. At eight o'clock, after five hours of walking, I still wasn't dilating. We went home. I took a sleeping

pill and went to bed. I had painful contractions all night
Wednesday as I lay in bed. I groaned so my husband suffered too.
I kept waking him up every three to five minutes. I wasn't fully
dilated until noon on Thursday. They never told me it would be
like this in the Lamaze class.

The birth itself was relatively routine. I had an epidural since I
had taken Pitocin to bring on the contractions. Afterwards, we
wondered why the birth had taken so long. Did I work out too
much? Perhaps I didn't exercise enough. I may have been afraid
of the birth and unconsciously wanted a delay. In retrospect I
think I just liked being pregnant and I didn't want to give up my
poolside partner.

My husband has been very good with the baby. He forces me out
the door to go swimming even though I hate to leave our child
even for two hours. If I have an appointment, he'll stay home. We
only fight over who gets to hold him. We've adjusted to our
baby's hours, which aren't too bad unless he stays up during the
day. At night I'll check to see if he's wet or I'll change him, and
in the morning I won't remember how many times I've been up.
Maybe I've learned to sleep on my feet. I love to breast-feed, and
I'd like to night and morning nurse him as long as possible.

I used to think I would pick up a script and return to work
immediately. Many of the scripts I'm reading would send me back
in two months to productions ranging from *Superman IV* to a TV
miniseries filmed in Morocco. I'm wondering, though, if I even

want a part right away. In going around to discuss prospective
roles, I always seem to bring around the conversation to my baby.
I can't help it. I dream of having four children and living on a
farm. I don't know how I'd ever tell my manager.

I've been doing two hundred situps a day to tighten my stomach,
and I have to begin making time for regular sessions in the pool's
fast lane. Like my sister, I expect I'll need six months healthy
diet and endless laps to lose the last few pounds.

I worry about taking my child onto a set in an exotic location and
finding myself overwhelmed by the combined acting, nursing, and
mothering. *Greystoke* and *St. Elmo's Fire* were fairly easy except
for the early mornings, but what about the Moroccan miniseries?
Television productions push hard to finish their shooting in
budget.

I'm actually at a strange age for an actress. At twenty-five or
twenty-six, roles are scarce. There are good parts for teenagers
and a lot of roles for older women, thirty to thirty-five, but few in
between. I haven't been ready to play an older woman, but
having a baby has aged me years inside; I'm better prepared each
day for those adult roles. When I broke from modeling, it felt
wonderful because I stopped thinking of myself as a pretty face.
If I take time off from acting for motherhood, my life will deepen
in the same way. I feel as if I've got my membership now in an
exclusive club and I plan on enjoying it. Acting can wait.

# PATRICIA SCHROEDER
. . . .

*Pat Schroeder is one of the most powerful women in Congress today. As the senior representative from Colorado, her strong stands on defense, employment, and women's issues have earned her a bipartisan reputation as an outspoken "fiscally conservative liberal." She challenges expensive military programs and champions parental leave, affirmative action, and a nuclear test ban treaty. Pat was first elected to Congress in 1972 and has been reelected six times since then. She is married to attorney James Schroeder. They have a son, Scott, and a daughter, Jamie.*

I'm probably the only person ever to be sworn into Congress with disposable diapers in my bag. Congress has had very distinguished single women and some who were widows, but virtually no congresswomen with young children. When I ran, I was convinced I'd lose, and that's the only reason I entered the race. We weren't prepared for victory and the family had to move almost overnight. We actually bought a house in Washington by phone!

Most political families are bumped one way or the other; they stay in Washington or they stay in their home district. Either way it's the politician who travels. Instead, our children became gypsies. Rather than spend money on the house or the car, I brought the children along. People were appalled that I took my children with me on business. Rather than seeing children as the future for this society, we treat them as a personal option to be left at home. I've been fortunate enough to have my children share my work, but the reality is that it's your job or your baby. Business has its priorities, and child care is low on the list. But business can help; parental leave would be a good start.

Parental leave means if you have or adopt a child, both parents are entitled to four months off work without pay. Except for Burkina Faso, Sudan, South Africa, Greenland, and Guinea, every other country in the world has done more. The Reagan administration claims parental leave will leave America uncompetitive in the world marketplace. That makes no sense. The nations knocking our socks off in trade already have parental leave.

Doctors now know that mother and child form their most important bonds in the first three months. They also hear from more and more young women who mentally divorce themselves from their babies before birth; these women are terrified of the pain of separation they'll face in going back to work. This is how the next generation of drug users is created. Instead of death penalties and additional jails, I'd rather see us spend money to bring up children the right way, in an environment that doesn't get them off to a wrong start. That's what programs like parental leave and latchkey day care are for.

Since World War II, our nation has trained generations of men into going to work and leaving women and children in female ghettos during the day. The contact between men and their children is missing. Women have become gatekeepers and interpreters between their husbands and children. We're orchestrating the breakup of the family, and white male politicians aren't trained to sense the issue. The most impressive sight of Jesse Jackson's campaign was the way he could do press conference after press conference with children crawling on his head and under his armpits while he juggled them and talked away. You never see a white male politician doing that. Children aren't part of their professional life.

I'm finding that women of my generation are beginning to believe that protecting their family doesn't stop with staying home and watching the children. They want to make government aware of crime in the streets, drug addiction, nuclear weapons—all the problems that bear on the safety of their family. Women of all ages are finding they have political power. There are more women voting than there are men. Women have the power and the authority to bring up the issues that concern them.

Women don't have a sense of their power, their ability to

influence legislation. Women will come up to me and talk about these issues, but they are afraid to approach men. The men aren't interested. Male politicians think there are no issues here because no one talks about them. And so it goes. Businesses will get ahold of their congressman and say, "We don't want that parental leave bill." I find that a young mother will stop pushing her stroller and say to me, "I really like your bill." That's terrific, but they should be talking to their representative. Career women especially shouldn't feel defensive about bringing up these issues at work or in the political arena. We feel we are supposed to be superwomen; we aren't allowed to complain about our workload. But we aren't superwomen; we're just equal.

I serve on the Armed Services Committee, and at hearings I ask generals and admirals about their biggest problem. They start in with "We need more tanks, we need more this—" I ask again, "What's your biggest problem?" They have one answer. Day care for the families of soldiers. Soldiers have a twenty-four-hour mission, and if you don't have around-the-clock day care, you're not ready for war twenty-four hours a day. These same generals and admirals are terribly reluctant to admit this. We have to persuade society that day care is as real and pressing a need as more military hardware or prisons. Men need to be taught that these are society's problems, not women's.

Nine years ago I took my children to a refugee camp in Thailand. What overwhelmed them was that no one they talked to had ever dreamed they would become refugees. The image we had was of peasants. Instead, we talked to professors, journalists, members of the royal family, people who spoke five or six languages. We asked them all, "How did you ever let this happen to yourself?" There is no explanation. Nobody can ever guarantee that you won't become a refugee. If you stay concerned, however, you'll be that much safer.

I thought my children would not want anything to do with public service, but they haven't been turned off. Scott is in Foreign Service School, and Jamie has run for office in school politics and has won. I've been lucky.

103

*Author Erica Jong's first novel,* Fear of Flying, *a candid look at female sexuality and sexual freedom, was a 1973 bestseller. She followed with the novels* How to Save Your Own Life *and* Fanny: Being the True Story of the Adventures of Fanny Hackabout Jones, *the collections* Witches *and* Parachutes and Kisses, *and* Megan's Book of Divorce *for children. Erica has also written five books of poetry. She and her daughter live in New York City.*

*F*anny was a book of advice from a mother to a daughter and a presentiment of what I wanted in my own life. Its heroine was a redheaded, blue-eyed horse-loving woman who stood for the daughter I saw for myself. I was thirty-two, and all I thought about was a child. My writing, my poetry was filled with this tremendous preoccupation. I had begun to adopt every stray dog I found. It was easier to have a baby than to continue rescuing all those animals. I seem to foretell events in my own life through my writing. The heroine I saw in *Fanny* was the child I gave birth to. Perhaps it's simply a case of being in tune with your subconscious as a writer.

I kept my pregnancy a secret while I toured for *How to Save Your Own Life.* Like most professional women, I felt I had no option. In this male-dominated society, my competence as a writer was on the line. I'm deeply sorry I never took a day off to enjoy my child. As a part of the superwoman generation of the seventies, I was out to display great feats of endurance. Nobody encouraged me to take a year off, nurse my baby, and get some rest. I just kept working through that horrendous first year. Society is not behind career women. On the contrary, we're told to keep it out of our professional lives. Don't go into the boardroom with milk leaking through your silk blouse. Keep pictures of your children off your desk. The President says, "If women want to have children, they will have to bear the brunt of it." Like him, we forget that children aren't a hobby; they're the next generation.

The world can wait while we sit home and nurse our children. War and peace will wait. Certainly, the *Phil Donahue Show* will wait a year for me. Instead, we're told not to take time off. If a year vanishes from your career, you'll never get back in. If I feel that way as a bestselling writer, imagine how an actress must feel when each passing year adds a line to her face? This is a cruel system. I had time to be ecstatic at birth, panic-stricken during the first week, and then I had time only for the superwoman mode.

Last year I plotted a TV series, wrote a book and several articles, renovated and ran my big house in the country, and dealt with my daughter's first year of school. I was under the curse of my life—earn an income, organize your activities.

One of the wonderful things about having a child is that you have to relinquish a certain amount of control. If you're an intellectual woman who has been concerned with ruling her life with her mind from adolescence on, the abdication of control is quite wonderful. It's part of God's miracle—the creation of independent life.

I once thought pregnancy and birth would be similar to the creative experience. This is why male artists always say that writing a book is like having a baby. It's not, and we live in a society that can't accept that the power of child-bearing makes women the stronger sex. Every woman in the world knows this, but we also know that if we want to have men in our lives, if we want to get ahead, we'd better not openly say it.

Molly will give me hell about working sometimes. When she was younger, she'd come into my room and say, "Stop writing, Mommy. We have enough money." She'd do all sorts of little

things to distract me, but I've never barred her from my studio. I like to write in the mornings when I'm fresh and I used to go right to work with a cup of coffee in my hand after getting up, but today, I have breakfast with Molly and see her off to school. I would prefer to roll out of bed and write in the dream state, but I can't. So I adapt.

When you're raising your child, you have wonderful companionship, and then you learn to give them up and let them go. I made a decision very early on that I didn't want her going through life dreaming of her absent father. When she wasn't even three, she was off to her father's house every weekend and I found that very wrenching. Still, Molly feels she has both parents and there's much more goodwill between me and my ex-husband.

I wrote *Megan's Book of Divorce* to explore how funny it was for a kid to be always missing some article of clothing or to have one dog at Mommy's and another at Daddy's. The problems of children caught in a divorce are so full of humor and pathos. I wrote the book for Molly as a bedtime story and she liked it. I found an illustrator I liked, and that's how it grew.

I only wish that mothers could fulfill their nature in a joyful way because society is so male-dominated, so antichild, antipregnancy, so antilife. For example, women are very sexy after having children, but who can find the time in a culture where women bear the brunt of raising children? We come into our full sexuality after giving birth. Childbearing gives us more blood vessels in the pelvis and stronger orgasms. The psychological aspect isn't easily measured, but we certainly begin to see the real value of our biology, of the hormonal and menstrual cycles that are such a nuisance when we're younger. We realize the true value of our bodies.

DEBBIE ALLEN

*Debbie Allen has received a Drama Desk Award and two Tony nominations*
*—one for the role of Anita in* West Side Story *and the other for Charity*
*in* Sweet Charity. *For the last six years, she has not only starred in the*
*television series* Fame *but has choreographed and directed the show. Her*
*other movie and television appearances include* Ragtime, Jo Jo Dancer,
*and* Roots: The Next Generation. *Debbie is married to NBA All Star*
*Norman Nixon. They have a daughter, Vivian.*

A large family was as normal a part of my life as singing and
dancing. My father and mother brought us up to be artists just as
a Texan tycoon would encourage his children to join the oil
business. My mother is a poet and an artist, and she was always
at the typewriter, thinking and working. We had to respect her
creativity and her need for space. At the same time she respected
us—we had as much freedom as we needed. In the early sixties
we wore our hair curly long before it was fashionable and we
turned vegetarian very early. I was meditating at the age of eight.
We were raised to be free minds and free spirits, and today all of
my brothers and sisters have their own place in music, drama, or
dance.

I couldn't wait to have children and continue the tradition. You
need to watch your children at a very early age for aptitude in
the fine arts, and you must have a plan for their development.
You can't let your children decide everything they want to do. My
daughter goes to dance class and she's going to get music lessons.
Very early in the morning, we play, read, and look at ballet tapes
together. She loves *The Nutcracker* for its story and imaginative
costuming. *Aurora's Wedding* with Margot Fonteyn and Nureyev is
wonderful, especially the part with Red Riding Hood and the
Wolf. I have to rewind, rewind, rewind that scene for her.

On a regular day we have our morning together, and then we eat
breakfast with her father. We share a bath, and if she's not going
to the park, if I'm not off for an exercise class or meeting, then

we just hang out. When I need to escape some stress, I cancel a meeting and we go somewhere, perhaps the zoo.

As a professional woman, I have to be aggressive about my work since my field—directing and producing—is dominated by men. I'm a woman and a mother, though, and my family comes first. If I were injured and my career ended, Vivian would still be there and I'd have to raise her. If all the autograph hunters went away, she would still love me. It's not a security blanket; it's a fact of life. Vivian is always more important than work. I once held up a performance of *Sweet Charity* for her because during intermission, she was upset and all she wanted was for Mommy to rock her to sleep. The audience simply had to wait another five or ten minutes and have another drink. I did the show and received a standing ovation.

I've worked very hard to get back in shape from my pregnancy, but I still have a lingering five pounds. The best remedy for me was standing in front of the mirror and talking to myself. "No, I don't want it! No! Oh no, baby, honey, you've got to fix that side up. Mount Everest is sagging, honey." You can't diet, especially if you're breast-feeding. I took long walks, started my pliés three weeks after, and I was dancing after three months. Stomach exercises were very important. When you have a child, every muscle in your body loosens up to let that baby out. Even if you're toned, the baby comes through like lightning through a wooded area. Swoosh! The trees are blown away. You have to put them back together, and that takes a lot of work. I bought an elastic band from a gym equipment shop, which stretches from under your breasts to the top of your hips. It's like a waist cincher, only rubberized and sweaty; it helps to tone the muscles.

During my pregnancy Norman and I toured Europe, and we went to Spain to see the Basques, the beautiful gypsies. They have TV in the remotest shanties, and they recognized me from *Fame.* We danced in the streets together, with Vivian inside me. Now I want to spend summers abroad, so Vivian can experience those moments for herself. I can't wait.

113

# L Y N N E  M E A D O W
· · · ·

*Lynne Meadow became the artistic director of the Manhattan Theater Club at twenty-five after graduating from the Yale Drama School. In her fifteen seasons since then, she has been responsible for some of the most stimulating and successful theater in New York.* Ain't Misbehavin', Mass Appeal, Crimes of the Heart, *and* Loot *all began at the MTC. Lynne herself has directed productions of* Ashes, Principia Scriptoriae, Sally and Marsha, Close of Play, *and* Body Poetry. *She is married to attorney Ronald Shechtman, and they have a son, Jonathan.*

I've worked in the theater for fifteen years; I've only been a mother for a year and a half. I have enormous confidence in my career, but I'm a wobbly-legged novice as a parent. Fortunately the two roles in my life aren't completely dissimilar. As a director I learn to trust actors as they grow into their roles. I don't command; I shape and guide their performance. It's a strange profession; actors have to be professional children. They pretend. They create. You watch your children the same way a director watches a cast. You observe and allow yourself to be guided by how the child is guiding you.

There is something so satisfying about just doing something with Jonathan. I give him a bath, or I take him swimming and it's enormously centering for me. What I love the most—if he will be quiet—is just to sit with him and let him drink his bottle and watch Dan Rather.

It was wonderful to be pregnant after working for over ten years and establishing myself in the theater. I didn't have to prove that I could do my job and was confident of my ability. I felt a calmness and a peacefulness about myself knowing what I can and can't do well and wasn't trying to grapple with achieving recognition from my peers.

I found many practical problems in slowing down enough to be a mother. I didn't work for a large corporation. I'd given my heart and soul to the Manhattan Theater Club. There was definitely an adjustment that had to be made and an understanding from the people that I worked with that I could be really committed to my work at the Manhattan Theater Club and I could also be a mother, and that those two things are not mutually exclusive. It was a little hard on everybody. Suddenly I had my own real child and I was taken away from people with whom I had worked so closely and exclusively all those years. I couldn't vanish on maternity leave and know that someone else would be filling my position.

It was frustrating to realize that for the first time in my life, my body was making demands on me that I couldn't override. If I was exhausted, really exhausted, more than I would be after spending two weeks in rehearsal preparing a show, I went to sleep. Nature wasn't asking for a discussion. I had to come to terms with my hormones, with mood swings from exhilaration to rage. I was trying to pursue my career, about which I feel very strongly, and I was forced home for naps. At first I was furious. Later I began to treasure the moments when I was forced to set aside my work for the child within. There's a reality the world should accept. Women shouldn't have to fight to say, "I can do everything at every moment as proficiently as a man." We have to acknowledge that motherhood will take you away from your career, and women shouldn't be penalized for it—just as men shouldn't be penalized for not having wombs.

I had twenty-six terrible hours of labor, and Jonathan was born prematurely. Two weeks later I began to hold meetings in my apartment. I breast-fed while we talked about next year's subscription campaign. It was a tumultuous time. The theater was moving, and we had to look for new office space. I once questioned an authority who thought women should take nine months off to be with their baby, and today I wonder why I ever doubted. I would have loved those months, but instead I went back to the office after ninety days. I did what I had to do for my theater, and I did the best I could with Jonathan, but "you can't do it all," as Katharine Hepburn once said.

I breast-fed Jonathan for three months, and we tried to get him on a schedule, but eventually he found his own feeding times. It took a long time before he regularly slept through the night. My husband would get up, and I'd find him occasionally at five-thirty in the morning blearily watching California women doing aerobic exercises on TV. This took heroism; he worked as hard as I did during the day.

The next season I had my best directorial effort in years, *Principia Scriptoriae.* The MTC had its strongest season in years, and I think there's a powerful argument to be made that if women have children, they go back to work with an enormously renewed sense of accomplishment and achievement. For me the renewed energy probably came from a concern that as a mother I wouldn't be able to aggressively pursue my career. I certainly proved to myself that I could work hard and still give Jonathan the time he needed.

Ron and I feel we've joined a club that everyone else has belonged to for years. The instant camaraderie between parents, the sense of oneness, is remarkable. We went out to dinner recently, and everyone discussed children, households, schools. I wasn't bored for a second. Once all that mattered was the first sound cue and how the lights came down at the end of the second act, or whether the playwright had understood the dynamics of the piece. Today I feel I've caught up to the rest of the world.

# J A N E  S E Y M O U R

. . . .

*British actress Jane Seymour made her acting debut in Richard Attenborough's film* Oh! What a Lovely War. *She has since starred in many film and TV productions, including* Captains and the Kings, Somewhere in Time, East of Eden, The Sun Also Rises, *and* War and Remembrance. *Her stage appearances include the role of Constanze Weber, the wife of Mozart, in Peter Shaffer's Broadway play* Amadeus. *She is married to her business manager, David Flynn. They have two children, Katie and Sean.*

I've always been sure that I was a very fortunate person with the right career, a wonderful man, and a blessed life. I was equally confident that a pregnancy was the one event that would never happen to me. I felt sure I'd need three or four years to conceive.

I was in the Broadway production of *Amadeus* when David and I decided upon marriage. We thought about how wonderful it would be to conceive on our honeymoon. We tried ahead of time, in March. I became pregnant immediately and left *Amadeus* because the theater was not insured for a pregnant actress on stage.

My father, an obstetrician and gynecologist, and my family arrived in time for the birth of Katie. They bent the rules at Cedar Sinai Hospital to let my father attend the birth, along with David. Thank goodness my father was there because his ideas were quite different from those of my doctors. I wanted the Lamaze method, but when I went directly into hard labor, my dear father suggested I have an epidural.

If I hadn't been given the epidural, I might have died. The baby had put her arm and shoulder through my rectal wall. This happens so rarely it's not written up in medical textbooks. As it was, I had a perfect child, I enjoyed the birth, and it felt nearly painless. I didn't know until afterwards that the doctor had to reconstruct my rectum. The video-camera tape is my proof of the

lack of pain. There's nothing there you couldn't show your vicar.

We've all been terrified into becoming martyrs for natural childbirth. My father told me, "You don't need to carry a cross for motherhood. Consider anything that will take away the agony, because after years and years of delivering babies, I know it doesn't have to be painful." Luckily for me, Sean's delivery was magnificent—and the epidural made it painless.

Two children close together are difficult. You worry about the psychological aspects. If I could ever recommend waiting to anyone, I'd advise them that the proper textbook interval is three and a half years. Katie has her own life, but she's very involved with Sean. She holds him, helps change him.

*121*

I made a rule about whether or not Katie should be in the public eye. I often go to England, and each time the paparazzi take photographs. Because of her extraordinary coloring, Katie stands out. It would be more traumatic for her to hide beneath a blanket or a coat, so I've given her a choice. Anytime she doesn't want to go through the publicity, she doesn't have to because she didn't choose my profession.

Breast-feeding Katie was the most rewarding experience of my life. When I stopped feeding her I returned to a normal relationship with my husband. I tried not to cut him out, but breast-feeding is not conducive to a great marriage. Both times I felt terribly depressed when I stopped.

After each pregnancy, I needed to be reassured by the industry by being hired again. One baby you get away with, but with two the moguls are convinced you'll be fat and matronly for the rest of your life. When I had Katie, I put on twenty-two pounds and within three weeks I was back to a size six for the Golden Globe Awards. They then gave me an amazingly bitchy, sexy, knock-'em-dead role to play. I couldn't resist. I told myself I'll have another baby and three months later I'll bring down the house. I did it and almost killed myself.

David and I work very hard, but we always play with the kids early in the morning. The family spends a good hour together, eating and talking, and in the evening we try to be there for some time together before bed. We'll tuck them in, sing to them, and all the rest. We've rented a house in Santa Barbara with horses, orange and avocado groves, a tennis court and swimming pool, and none of that Hollywood nonsense.

I didn't choose to do it all. I just couldn't live without having children. I can't live without a career. It's damned hard and full of compromises. I may not become the world's greatest, best-known, or most glorious and beautiful actress. I don't even know where we are going to live in a few years time. We might live in England or we might live in Santa Barbara. I do know that I can't imagine a better life.

My relationship with my husband is the most important priority in my life. An imperfect relationship leads to imperfect parents. Both of us come from good marriages and both of us have had divorces. We know how hard it is to keep it all intact, working as hard as we do. That's why we sometimes spend time away from the kids. Just the two of us. We'll be better parents for it. Motherhood has relaxed me in many ways. You learn to deal with crisis. I've become a juggler, I suppose. It's all a big circus, and nobody who knows me believes I can manage, but somehow I do.

# MARTHA LAYNE COLLINS
. . . .

*Martha Layne Collins was sworn in as Kentucky's first woman governor in*

*1983. She is only the third woman to be elected governor of a state*

*without succeeding her husband. After graduating from the University of*

*Kentucky, she taught home economics and mathematics until 1971, when*

*she began working in campaigns around the state. In 1975 she ran for her*

*first office, and four years later she became Kentucky's lieutenant governor.*

*In 1984 Governor Collins served as chairman of the National Democratic*

*Convention. She is married to Dr. Bill Collins and has two children,*

*Stephen and Marla.*

When I was elected governor in 1983, we quickly moved into the governor's mansion in Frankfort, Kentucky. Our possessions were still in boxes as the legislature met for the new year. On one particularly busy day, as I stood before the state senate, a staff member ran up to me with a note. Was there a surprise parliamentary maneuver brewing down on the floor? I began to worry. I opened the note. It read, "Mom, where are my cheerleading shorts?"

You don't drop into politics after your children are grown up and moved away. Successful politicians put in many hours over many years. I remember a headline for the election of the only other woman in Kentucky to make it to lieutenant governor: "Thelma Stoval Wins After 25 Years Paying Dues." I could move up more rapidly because she had been there before me, but I worked very, very hard, starting from nowhere—a degree in home economics. No law school, no doctorate. Inevitably it was tough on my family. I couldn't just go to an office, work, and come home.

Balancing career and family has meant setting a series of priorities. Marla was a cheerleader, and I didn't see her cheer every game. My kids have been in plays that I've missed. I've picked them up from school and taken them to countless fish fries and church suppers where they listened to speeches they'd long since memorized. Steve and Marla lived through mudslinging campaigns, and always they've been under public scrutiny.

Today they tell me they understand and it didn't really matter that so much of their self-sufficiency and maturity had to come early. They sound very sincere. I don't have any trouble believing them because I know the opportunities they've had. They've already seen more of Kentucky than most adults. When I chaired the Democratic National Convention several years ago, Steve was the chairman of the Kentucky delegation. He did very well. He was a constitutional page at the Kentucky senate several times, and that taught him parliamentary procedure. It's been a tremendous practical education for him. He has a tremendous knack for people and names. He's wonderful with the elderly. I don't doubt his experiences have had something to do with it.

One of the things that's helped me with the kids is the sense of history we all feel from day to day. As the first woman governor of Kentucky I'm entering the history books in a small way, and I hope I'm making some sort of a lasting impact on Kentucky's direction for the future. Steve and Marla were brought up very patriotic, very loyal to the Commonwealth and their part in my

career and politics means a great deal to them. I hope they're
aware of their own contribution to this state.

I don't think I could manage raising a family now. I'm usually in
the office by eight, and the workday runs right through social
functions or meetings in the evening. My husband is often out
traveling around the state. Steve and Marla visit often; I depend
on them for assistance with events at home—arranging the menus
and all the details that go into a formal dinner. We don't see each
other as often as we'd like, but we do try to have dinner together
a minimum of once a week, a meal where we can sit together and
not be rushed. The weekends always seem to be filled up; they're
full of festivals and parades, and I'm out there meeting people.

I like to think that even if I haven't always been there for them,
I've taught them by example what my parents taught me: You're
put on this earth for a purpose and you'd better be able to
account for your time. In flying to functions around the state, I'll
glance out the window at a house and wonder who lives there and
how my decisions affect them. I want my children to ask those
same questions. I work as hard as I can at being a good governor.
I hope they'll bring the same sense of purpose to their lives.

# P A T T I  L a B E L L E
· · · ·

*In 1977, after eighteen years as a lead singer with the Ordettes,*

*Bluebelles, and LaBelle, Patti LaBelle went solo. In 1982 she starred on*

*Broadway and then toured the country in* Your Arms Too Short to Box

with God. *Since 1985 her career has been on a meteoric rise. Her latest*

*album went gold before it reached the stores. She was born in West*

*Philadelphia and married Armstead Edwards, a high school principal.*

*They still live in Philadelphia with their son Zuri and adopted sons*

*Stanley and Dodd.*

My son was made in Japan. Laura Nyro took us there, and on the very first night we conceived our son. She is his godmother and takes full responsibility for his presence in this world. He was made in Japan and born in Philadelphia. A few weeks after he came home from the hospital, Laura would come and sing to him from under the tree in front of our house. She has a big voice, and the lullaby would drift into the house and she would come in when he fell asleep.

When I found out I was pregnant, I told my manager and LaBelle that I would just have to keep singing. I sang until I was eight months pregnant, had a painless delivery, and two months later I was back on the road. My husband stayed with Zuri, and when I had a day off, I'd come back home, stay up all night, and cry. I was so tired. I gritted my teeth and told myself there were people worse off.

Zuri was about five when we adopted our other two sons, Dodd and Stanley. Dodd moved in first. His mother, our neighbor, wasn't a close friend at all—I would see her coming from work— she was a very beautiful lady. She had no idea when she was living that I would end up taking two of her sons if anything ever happened to her! When she died, I said to Dodd, "Bring over your clothes and bring your brother."

It wasn't a natural thing to do. I wondered if we would love them as much as we did Zuri. I didn't want anyone to be in my house feeling that they weren't loved, and I didn't want them ever to feel we would do more for Zuri than we would for them. After they were with us for a while, we realized that we did love them as much and that it wasn't one-sided; we just had to give it a chance. We look like a family and we are a family. They are not show business kids and do not brag that Patti LaBelle is their mother, which I like very much.

I was lucky to be in a family that was well provided for. My father was a railroad worker and my mother was a homemaker. We were fortunate to eat three meals a day and wear some clothes sometimes that weren't hand-me-downs.

I was twelve when they separated and I couldn't understand it. I broke out in hives, it made me nervy. I thought, "Why me?" I thought we had a perfect family. When you are a kid, you think things are perfect. You see them hugging and kissing—but you don't know what is going on when the doors are closed . . . boxing maybe!

My mother used to give me a nickel to go out to play with the kids. I didn't go out. I was afraid of people. My friends were animals, little butterflies, and my cat and dog. I felt confident with them. My confidence increased as I grew older, but I am still very shy, like Zuri. I used to say to my father, who used to sing in clubs, that I would sing "rings around him." My parents were not pushy show business people.

I miss my family when I am on tour, and I end up calling home three times a day. By the end of the trip, I've spent the price of a plane ticket and I could have had Zuri with me. But it is better if he stays in school. He is very athletic and is center for the basketball team.

I worry whether they are eating right, but my husband is a good cook and he makes sure they get wonderful food—I feel that is my job and I would like to be able to cook for them more than I do. My cooking is a way of sending love and affection over the stove. If Zuri has a friend over, he will impress him by letting him taste his mother's cooking. I even cook on tour, something like shrimp accompanied by my famous Stringbeans Patti LaBella —steamed string beans with fresh tomatoes, garlic, oregano, and Provolone cheese on top.

We were on the only tour bus in the country with a stove, and as it drove across country, I juggled twenty chickens with grease spattering across my arms. Armstead held the frying pan while I diced and sauteed a cabbage with green peppers, onions, and oil. My backup singers, the Sweeties, diced and sliced. Nina Blackwell from MTV helped. The bus driver had to stop on every other corner to let us throw dirty water out.

I finally ended up strolling through K-Mart in heels and a nightshirt to find another electric fry pan. I enjoyed showing Zuri that I could cook under any circumstances. He asked me, "Is this the best?" It's a game we play between us; any given meal is always the best. We fed over fifty people.

Zuri would rather have a normal mother, someone who isn't held up by photographers or autograph sessions. He is very good at spotting the users, the people who are around me only because I am Patti LaBelle, a singer they can take advantage of. He will let them know what he thinks; he is very open with his feelings, and I love that about him because I am very passive, very forgiving. Zuri is very honest. He will give his side of a problem, how he thinks it should be solved.

We didn't plan for a Made in Japan baby, but we are glad it happened. I am a more conscientious caring person because of my son. If my husband and I argue, Zuri stands between us and one look from his eyes makes us chill out. He holds us together.

*Georgette Klinger developed her skincare techniques during study at the universities of prewar Europe. In 1940 she came to New York and opened her first Georgette Klinger salon. Currently she and her daughter Kathryn run salons in New York, Beverly Hills, Dallas, Palm Beach, Chicago, and Bel Harbor. Georgette is well known for her philanthropy and involvement in professional women's organizations. Since 1977 Kathryn has been director of the company, which grosses over $13 million each year.*

I was thirty-five when I had Kathryn. I thought it was a miracle for me to have a baby. She was a surprise. I dreamed of having a baby, but I didn't think I was still young enough to have one. It was the biggest miracle that ever happened. Nobody could tell I was pregnant until the end. I just wore a size larger dress. Now the outlook of our pregnant clients is a far different one. We hid our stomachs. This generation is proud of them. The whole outlook today is a happier one.

135

. . . .

There was not one day that my daughter Kathryn complained when she was pregnant with my grandson Trevor, and she returned to work one week after having him!

I had a special beauty regimen when I was pregnant. I was always afraid of sagging so I used creams, lotions, and masks. I had regular massages, which I hated. The creaming was so terribly important. I see it in my customers who look after their skin. Pregnancy definitely changes the skin.

Kathryn was brought up by a governess and I spent all my vacation time with her. My husband was a Venezuelan citizen. His business was there so we would pick him up on a boat and vacation together in Europe or at Lake Placid. It was an important thing for me to vacation with my husband and Kathryn.

When Kathryn was a little baby, I spent most of my time with her. When she started school, everybody I knew told me to be there when she came home. Well, I wasn't because that was our closing time and that was the time when people told me their problems. It was difficult for me. I was torn and always felt guilty about not being with my child. I think I should have been there when she came home from school. The moment she started her education, I started to rebuild my business. It had grown so large so quickly that I had to move.

136

I had started my business in the 1940s and it was a terrific struggle the first year I started. It was during the war and all my friends said, "Don't do it, it is impossible. You can't succeed because you can't get jars and raw material," and of course it wasn't a mistake because my products were badly needed. My name took on very quickly because nobody in America knew about skin care—you could get a facial at a beauty parlor and that was it.

I never thought of myself as ambitious, I never wanted great things, just help in the house because washing dishes doesn't make me happy. I go in circles when I have to clean. Being in business changed me, and experience is the best teacher. Of all my experiences the most wonderful has been motherhood; just having the love of a child and being able to give all that love.

Kathryn was very fond of her governesses and was strong enough to let me know if she didn't like them. One was English and spoiled her too much. I made the big mistake of letting her go. I wanted a French governess so that Kathryn would be bilingual. Of course this didn't work. You see the mistakes afterwards. In retrospect, I believe my biggest mistake was that I wasn't there when she came home from school. I should have been home.

Kathryn grew up with the business. Most kids played with toys; she played with cosmetics. She began coming in after school, putting stamps on mail-order packages when she was six, and worked her way up to telephone answering by the age of twelve. After college she started full time.

One day everybody at the salon was sick. There wasn't even a receptionist. I said, "Can you please come in for the day, answer the telephones, and take the clients to their rooms?" That is how she got into the business. She was twenty-two years old.

Kathryn is very organized and I am very disorganized. She got stuck in the business because she was so good at it. I have never known whether Kathryn came in just to please me. It was never clear. She had other talents and it was a great surprise when she decided.

We are very close. Even with Kathryn living in Beverly Hills, we talk every day at least once, partly business and partly just talking. Now we're working together.

# DEBBY BOONE

· · · ·

*In 1977 Debby Boone's recording of "You Light Up My Life" stayed at the number one position in the* Billboard *record chart for an unprecedented ten weeks. The single ultimately sold over four and a half million copies and won an Oscar as the year's best original song. Debby won a Grammy that same year as best new artist. Since then she has released four other solo albums and four albums with her sisters. She won another Grammy in 1980 for her album* With My Song. *In addition to her music, she starred in several television specials and movies, and she coauthored a 1981 autobiography,* Debby Boone—So Far. *She and her husband, Gabriel Ferrer, have four children—Jordan, twins Gabrielle and Dustin, and baby Tessa.*

I was pregnant one month after I was married. I'm actually glad I was forced into motherhood because I could never have had a convenient pregnancy as my career progressed. I am relieved to think that I'll have had all my kids before I was thirty. On the other hand I love large families, and as the girls have been getting older, I have been asking myself, "Am I ever going to have this experience again?"

My pregnancies haven't been easy. Why does anyone ever choose to spend six months throwing up and gaining weight? Fortunately the third time around was an improvement. In my second pregnancy, I didn't know I was having twins until the seventh month. I asked for a sonogram because I had started hard contractions. My doctor told me I was overreacting. He was so embarrassed by the sonograms, which showed two babies side by side, heads down, that he came to our doorstep the next day to tell me the news. I simply said, "You're kidding," but Gabri sat down with a magazine to avoid fainting. The idea was immensely frightening to both of us.

I didn't know what to expect, having twin babies. Delivering and raising two babies was scary to me. It was like the shock of finding out that I was pregnant for the first time. There was so much to think about. I wasn't prepared.

I bloomed straight out. I stopped traffic. In restaurants hostesses said, "Please don't have your baby in this restaurant." I waited through a very hot August with my ankles swollen beyond all proportion. At night I prayed to God to not let me wake up still pregnant. Swimming saved me—I floated and let the water hold my weight. There must have been twenty-five people in the delivery room, the hospital took the birth of twins so seriously.

Gabrielle was born first and Dustin was delivered next with the cord wrapped around her neck. All those nurses and doctors, and no one knew where the scissors were. Dustin began to turn blue and the staff began to panic. Fortunately somebody came up with the scissors. Gabri almost fainted dead away—he was white for three days after. I recovered before he did. I recently went to watch my sister have her first; the breathing and pushing made me extremely nervous. I felt a bit of what Gabri went through.

I couldn't have got through these years without my husband. My friends have to walk on tiptoes to ask if their husbands will watch the baby. Gabri will be there when I'm not. I love for him to go away and have fun, even if I am there for the weekend with kids. I know he'll reciprocate. Most men can't define what their duty should be as a father.

I want to have answers for my kids. I want to raise them the best that they can possibly be raised. The things that used to be important to me aren't anymore. Work is not that important. I love what I do and that I have the opportunity to do what I do, but it never, ever takes precedence over what is good for them and our marriage.

The only time I feel comfortable is when I feel I am not sacrificing the needs of my kids because of my work. I think people still see me as Pat Boone's daughter instead of somebody's mother. I think the children in some way help my image, juggling the career and all the responsibilities of raising four kids. I certainly don't take anyone lightly who does all that. I am not just Pat Boone's daughter who coasted in on his success.

J U L I A  M I G E N E S - J O H N S O N
· · · ·

*Born in Manhattan of a Puerto Rican mother and a Greek father, Julia Migenes-Johnson began playing children's roles in operas at the age of three. She received her first rave notices as Maria in a 1964 revival of* West Side Story. *She studied and worked in Europe, developing her operatic career and performed with leading companies of Vienna, Paris, San Francisco, and Houston. In 1980 she starred in Berg's* Lulu *at the Metropolitan Opera. Her performance as Carmen in Francesco Rosi's film* Carmen *has brought her international acclaim. She lives in Great Neck, New York, with her two children, Martina and Jessica.*

Y ou have to overcome yourself to be a mother. I had to learn to separate children and career. I had to perform. If I couldn't, I was paralyzed. I would fall into a sort of apathy. At the same time, I learned that if you're watching over a sick kid, you can't be too serious about singing for people; you go on stage, but it's not as important as the child at home. Still, during the same evening, I would be on stage, doing my job, and suddenly I would forget the pain. I would sing.

It isn't always easy as a mother to remain an artist. I nursed Jessica, my second baby, for ten months. She wanted to drink every two hours day and night. I had tours, singing at the Met and in Houston, and she would never sleep! I was too tired to get up when she wanted to nurse. She slept in my arms, and I hung my breasts out in case she was thirsty. I wanted to breast-feed her myself, and I didn't want to use the pump.

Still, I'm a beautiful mother when my art is rich and wonderful. I use the instincts of the stage to make my child happy. Last night I sang Schumann to Jessica and she said, "Sing the 'Baby Song.'" The "Baby Song" came from when I was on tour and still nursing her. I remember the two of us in bed, my music spread in front of me: I was singing, "When my baby smiles at me, I go to Rio." She loves it still. Martina used to sing all my

difficult arias, exaggerating my vibrato, which I didn't particularly care for.

Martina's father was a ballet dancer, a beautiful young Ukrainian who taught me how to knit. I thought Daniel was safe, but he wasn't. He did love me, and his caring and devotion gave me the strength to have a child.

We never married. When Martina was two and a half, we separated, and it was very difficult for her because she was so close to her father. When I had to tour, I boarded the plane to Vienna with Martina and two turtles in a pail, dropped her off with him for a month or two, picked her up with the turtles, and continued on.

Everything changed when I met my third husband, Jervis. Daniel felt sure I was going to sweep Martina off to America forever, and he tried for custody. I asked my lawyer, "If I were to walk away with her, what could he do? What is possession?" "Possession," he said, "is the person who happened to have her at the moment." Can you imagine? You could fight for years to get your child back just because it was sitting on the other person's lap.

Jervis had a plan. If I came out of the hearing and gave a signal, he would run and stop everybody while I grabbed her and sprinted to a car waiting around the corner. But so much for drama; I won the case.

Because I was marrying and moving to America, Daniel kidnapped her back. I took him to court by telling a terrible lie. The court said, "Of course, she is his." I said firmly, "I don't remember." And so I took him to court when otherwise I might not have been able to see Martina for five years.

When I got her back, Martina had been hidden in another country. She was now four and a half years old, and she instinctively felt that I had robbed her best years of love. We'd missed so much together. For example, I felt extremely guilty that I'd never suckled her. We never had the emotional bonding

146

nursing builds between woman and child. I knew I would have to
be as docile as a cow. As soon as I became agitated and angry,
she would clam up. The confrontations were terrible.

I knew that anything you put in a child will stay there, like a
computer. I was aware of how my upbringing shaped me for my
music. I was absolutely unscholastic; I couldn't read until I was
ten. My childhood gave me a street intelligence. I learned four
languages by ear. As a mother, I knew I held the same power
over Martina and Jessica's potential that my mother's upbringing
held over me.

My first instinct was to be like my mother. She brought me up in
an environment where you never knew when somebody would fly
off the handle, throw something, scream. The drunkard my
mother lived with turned on the gas to kill us. My mother hid the
knives. She broke milk bottles over his head because he took an
ice pick to her. I escaped by singing. The stage was the real

147

world. I had to unlearn my past for Martina. I held a deep and fundamental desire to step beyond my limitations, to meet the responsibility.

I get up with my children in the morning, spend two hours in the afternoon with them, and put them to bed. If I am singing in the evening, we eat breakfast together; I work at arranging those odd moments. If the job is important and the money available, I take them with me just so we can steal five minutes, a few seconds, together.

I love those small exhilarating moments the child gives to you! The hours when both of them are playing together, or the afternoon Jessica came to me singing, "I'm bringing home a baby bumblebee," and performed her song with hand movements. Or the time I watched Martina dance and saw revealed in her an artist's grace and style. Those small, quiet moments.

# A C K N O W L E D G M E N T S

*Without the help and forbearance of our loving husbands, Kevin and Harry, this book would never have been completed.*

*Thank you to Paul Bresnick, our editor, whose interest in motherhood and fatherhood truly made this book possible.*

*To Lorin Klaris, photo assistant, for her help in assisting through all the shootings, and printing the fifteen hundred work prints for this book.*

*To Barbara Sahlman, the gracious hostess who introduced us; Madeleine Morel for putting us in contact with Paul Bresnick.*

*To Geni Guerrero, Lena Belcourt, Claude Saunier, and Sophie van Loock for their help with our children.*

*To Klaus Moser and his laboratory for the processing and contact sheets of all the film, and Carol Dilley for doing the final prints for the book.*

*To Doug Lloyd for his great help with the design and production of the book.*

*To Al Lowman, our agent, and to Doug Meurs for his help with the editing. To Richard Mealey for transcription. To Kevin Lein, Tamara Hendershot, Tara Shannon, Robin Leach, Catherine Olim, Rob Cohen, Beth Handler, Joel Brokaw, Billie Deeson, Gina Silvester, Ira Sahlman, Marcie Bloom, Peggy Silhanek, Larry Mitchell, and Ruth Ansel.*

*A special thanks to Treat Williams, who took two days out of his vacation to fly us up and down the East Coast. And to Chevy Chase for lugging all the camera equipment at the airport.*

*Most important, to all the women who invited us into their homes to meet their children and be a part of this book.*